*A Dreaming Spires Revision Guide:*

# HOW TO AC

# ENGLISH LANGUAGE

# IGCSE

## *(0500 CIE VERSION HIGHER TIER)*

*Eight Lessons to Get a Grip!*

# CONTENTS

# FOREWORD

Hello and welcome to this revision course to help prepare for the CIE 0500 English Language iGCSE (higher tier) exam.

This revision guide is a book-format version of the popular crammer course taught online as Dreaming Spires Revision. It is not affiliated with the Cambridge International Examinations board in any way, but just the observations, tips, and ideas based on my many years of experience with this exam.

Normally, I don't like teaching to an exam. I think it does a disservice to any subject; however, I have observed mistakes that students make again and again both in my own tutees' work and via numerous online resources. I started creating a list of do's and don'ts[1] which grew over time into an

---

1 This looks a badly punctuated phrase, but after researching many options for it, I chose this as the clearest one.

online revision course, and finally, into this little book.

It just seems that, if students are going to be taking this exam, they deserve to know the best way to do it.

Besides, I've come to accept that in education, as in any journey, students need to not only buy the ticket, but they probably want to buy one that's the most direct route, as well.

This revision guide is like going "as the crow flies" on your journey: as direct a route as you can get!

Here, you will find tips and tricks that will help you manage your stress, your time, and your approach, and therefore, you should do better on it having worked through its exercises.

Of course, there are no guarantees. People

underperform for so many reasons — bad time management, failure to read the question, preparing only the exam papers rather than learning the general skills, or just blind panic.

This guide is here to minimise such mistakes, and help you toward the best exam answers you can make. I admit it's rough around the edges, this book, but the information is what matters: I hope you can forgive the idiosyncratic formatting!

Finally, you might want to pop on over to Facebook and get connected with other students who are using this revision guide, past students of the online courses, or even yours truly. Communication is key. We might not solve the world's problems, but hopefully, we'll crack the revision approach to 0500 together.

Many regards,

Dr P

# BEFORE YOU BEGIN

*Know that there's no rush.*

First of all, if you have bought this book before you know how to write a good sentence, before you know how to paragraph, spell reasonably well, write with a decent vocabulary; before you have read a lot of good books; and before you have some maturity (usually, but not always, this is after you're 14), then I think you should really go away and practise, read, and live a bit more.

Harsh, but remember — I have a lot of experience with this exam. I read a lot of papers every year, and I can tell when someone is too young, whose skills are too weak, whose knowledge is limited, and this person may struggle for having sat this exam too soon. The bulk of students sitting this exam are 15 or 16, maybe even 17, so if you take it earlier than that, I believe you may be taking an unnecessary risk.

So, in my opinion, you should wait. It will only do you favours!

*Know that there's due diligence involved.*

You can buy the book and never crack it open. Or you can thumb through it. Or you can work on it for an hour or so, but if you're serious about your studies, you will set aside regular time to concentrate, to practise, and to expect to learn something.

Whichever you choose, it makes no difference to me: once you've bought it, I've got my reward for the work I've put into this guide for you.

Your reward comes in August after you've taken exams, when your grade arrives.

I don't know about you, but my personal

feeling is that I'd like to know I did my very best when I open that list of marks and see what I made. I would be very cross with myself if I thought I could have done better, if only I'd worked a bit harder in the Spring.

*Know that there are expectations.*

Finally, I require all my revision students to commit to a regular homework regime of basic skills. Decide for me right now that you're going to do this, on your own, regularly and diligently.

Are you ready to make that decision?

Assuming you said yes, then you have committed to improving your test-taking skills and writing ability that will make you a better student and, yes, even a better person.

Expectation one:

Four times a week, you will copy out this

19.2.18

7

sentence:

*It is as important to read and understand the question as it is to read and understand the unseen reading passages.*

I refer to this as the "memory verse". Most of the time that students bomb a question, it's because they didn't read it carefully enough.

Over the years, my former students come back to tell me that this was such a great bit of advice, and that memorising this verse has served them well in all their subjects, all their exams.

So, during this revision course that you're committing to here, you could write this verse down as many as 36 times. Get one of those little exercise books from W H Smiths and keep it for only this purpose.

Expectation two:

Another regular task you will do four times a week is called copywork. This is a Charlotte Mason method staple, but it's also crucial you do this for the exam — it will improve your vocabulary, sentence structures, punctuation, and reading comprehension. The sooner you get started, the more effect it will have on your writing style.

Here's the task: choose a really good book like Dickens' A Tale of Two Cities or Lord of the Rings or something really dense and wordy. Set your timer for ten minutes, and then carefully copy a passage word for word, making sure every word is spelled correctly, every punctuation mark is perfect.

Over time, you will probably find that you can hold four or five words in your head at a time as you copy them out, but just remember: this is supposed to be ten minutes of perfection, so don't rush, and don't lose concentration.

## Expectation three:

In Lesson One, you will see something called "narration" — this is just a summary of what you've read, but it works on the deep-memory of your brain and makes it "stick" more. Getting in the habit of narrating everything you read will contribute to a stronger understanding of the unseen passages you get in the exam. As part of exam technique, I suggest that students read a paragraph of the passage, jot a little marginal marker about what it said, and move to the next paragraph, doing the same.

If you start doing this technique for EVERYTHING your read — whether it's science textbooks, novels, the newspaper —

it will help you improve your attentiveness while you're reading, and thus, improve your comprehension.

Summary:

So, you have now committed to doing three things on a regular basis: copying the memory verse 4 times a week, doing 10 minutes of copywork for 4 days a week, and narrating everything you read regardless the subject.

These three tasks, performed regularly and diligently, will be the first thing that sets you apart from 99% of the students who sit this exam.

Don't you want to be in the top 1% before you even sit down in the exam centre???? Of course you do!

Finally, there are occasional exercises in each lesson, demarcated by the instruction

"DO" and followed by a little symbol that looks like this:

*DO NOT PROCEED*
*without doing the task first*

As he says, you are not to proceed any further in the book until you have done the task. Revision isn't revision if you just read through it — you have to put into practice what I'm telling you, or you might as well have bought two tall vanilla lattes and a slice of cheesecake from Starbucks instead of spending the money on this book. (Instead, I'll be buying the lattes BECAUSE you bought this book — thank you very much.) Seriously: do the exercises.

# How to Use this Book

Ideally, you will work through this revision guide over an eight-week period. I think there's a lot to take on board if you try to do it faster, and sometimes, you just need to let ideas, skills, and advice to sink in before trying to put more ideas, skills, and advice into the mix. It is possible, however, to do a lesson every day, as I do in my online crammer, for a total of eight days.

Each of the eight sessions is set out in the same format: a review, a quiz, an overview, a look at something specific, and revision suggestions.

I strongly advise that you get a blank book and actually take notes from the guide. Studies show that students learn better by writing notes by hand because it requires more connections in the brain, and thus, helps digest the information more.

Now an apology: I'm sorry that there is a blurred-out image or two in the guide. No, there's nothing wrong with your eyes, and there's nothing wrong with my printer. I've had to blur out the images because they belong to CIE, and I don't have the legal right to reproduce them. I can only give you the impression of what they say or look like, so you will need to hunt down a copy of the exam papers yourself. My suggestion is that you look on **xtremepapers.com**. Print these out so you have them to refer to.

While on the subject of copyright, please note that this book is copyrighted, too. That means that you don't have any right to reproduce this guide, print it out, or share it, so please respect that in an honourable way. The photos, too, are mine, unless otherwise noted.

Now that's enough preliminary chit-chat; let's get started, and good luck!

# LESSON ONE

As we start this revision course, I want to set the record straight about something. I don't actually believe in the old proverb "practice makes perfect".

Just think of how many ways you could disprove that. Say, I play the piano and I plink-plonk away at the keys for 2 hours a day, blissfully unaware that my version of Fur Elise is missing the all-important D-sharp. All I've done is made permanent my imperfection. In other words ...

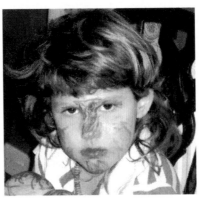

Practice doesn't make perfect ...
It makes permenant!

What I mean in terms of your revision is that you shouldn't rush this process, but take your time in learning the basics and the underlying principles, and then you will have a firm grasp of what's expected. The more your practise slowly at first, getting everything right from the beginning, the more confidence you'll gain, and eventually, the faster you'll be able to manage the exam paper.

## 0500 Higher Tier at a Glance

The English (First Language) iGCSE exam is made up of three papers, each with various codes. Paper 1 is the Core level paper; I don't cover it in this course. I do cover the other two papers — generically, they're known as 0500-02 and 0500-03, but you are probably taking 0500-22 and 0500-31. Papers can also be coded 21 or 23, 32 or 33, and that's because the exam board creates several different versions so those in countries with wildly different time zones can take their exam while not spoiling the questions for people whose time zone means they take the exam later.

There's also an exam taken by students in India in February/March of each year, also with the codes 0500-22 and -32. If you can find a copy of them on the internet, they're useful for revising and taking as a mock.

The difference between the two papers is the emphasis: Paper 2 is the READING paper, and Paper 3 is the WRITING paper.

Don't think for a minute that you don't need to do any writing in Paper 2, nor any reading in Paper 3. That's not what I mean. It's a matter of emphasis, though, and Paper 2 is more concerned with your reading comprehension, ability to read between the lines, and understand how language works;

while Paper 3 is more concerned with your ability to organise your writing and demonstrate some level of skill in terms of vocabulary, punctuation, spelling, and the like.

We'll look more at the writing paper starting in Lesson 5. Until then, we'll focus on the reading paper, and more specifically, from 0500-22 from the summer 2015 exam.

GENERAL POINTS ABOUT the 0500-22 (or other Paper 2 versions)

0500-22 is the reading paper and contains TWO PARTS:

Part One refers to Passage A from the insert, and two questions.

Part Two refers to Passage B from the insert, and one question in two parts.

That's THREE questions in total based on TWO unseen passages. You are required to answer ALL THREE questions.

**DO: Look at the front page of your question paper and notice where it says "Answer ALL questions in the space provided." Underline that and write "All" in the margin with an arrow to the same word.**

The first part of the paper is based on Passage A from the insert:

Question 1: a writing task to prove you understand the passage, and use the information to change audience and purpose

Question 2: a task of analysis to prove you can understand how language works

20

## _Key idea = careful reading_

The second part of the paper is based on Passage B:

Question 3a: list 15 salient points from the passage about a topic they give you;

Question 3b: taking these points and put them into your own words in summary form.

## _Key idea = Choices!_

NOTE: Question 3 needs you to really pay attention to what topic it's asking you to pull out of Passage B. This is where your Memory Verse training comes in handy.

Remember the memory verse from "How to Use this Book"?

**It's as important to read the question and comprehend what it wants as it is to read and comprehend the unseen passages!**

## SUMMARY ABOUT PAPER 2

The Reading Paper, 0500-22, contains 3 questions. It wants to analyse your ability to read and understand the unseen materials, to manipulate the information, to analyse the language of the writing, and pinpoint key details.

**IT ALSO REQUIRES THAT YOU READ THE QUESTIONS CAREFULLY!!!**

DETAILED STUDY OF 0500-22 from Summer 2015

- •We are going to look at Passage A
- •We are going to talk about the best way to gain understanding about the passages in the inserts; this is a fundamental step that many students miss out.
- •We will talk about Question 1 specifically in Lesson 2.

**DO: Read through Passage A from the insert about Zelda and Bob's canal holiday.**

After reading that passage, I want to go over how you should THINK about the inserts for the exam.

Let me say first of all that my own home-education philosophy is based on a method popularised by Charlotte Mason, a pioneering educator during the Victorian period.

One of the hallmarks of her method is something called "narration". I mentioned this skill in "Before you Begin" under Expectation Three.

"Narration" is simply a telling back of what you've read. It sounds so easy, but the process your brain goes through is such that you remember a passage much better if you put into words what you've been reading. This is so much more successful a way of remembering than having short-answer quizzes or multiple choice.

So let's try it. I am NOT assuming you'll be any good at this if you've never done it before; however, I KNOW that you will be jolly good at it by the time the exam comes round in May, because you are going to practise doing it as part of your revision for this exam, and for every exam or subject you're studying now.

1 **DO: Read the first two paragraphs of Passage A from the insert, and then without looking at the passage any more, write down a summary of the**

**paragraphs in your notebook.**

It's very important that you don't look back at the passage, because you are trying to teach yourself to *attend to* the passage as you read it, rather than being lazy and referring back to it as a crutch.

After you have done this activity, then you may go to the answer section and read my version.[1] Remember, mine is only one example of many, so don't feel bad if yours isn't exactly the same.

That's what a normal narration looks like. But you're not going to do a "normal" narration in the exam. You don't have time. Instead, you're going make use of something I call "**marginal markers**".

Marginal markers are very short narrations — say, a word or a phrase — that you'll jot down next to each paragraph as a way of reminding yourself what each paragraph is about. This will help you find things faster when you're writing your answers, but at the same time, it serves as additional comprehension for yourself as you read through the unseen passages on the insert.

Mini-narrations, in other words.

Here's an example:

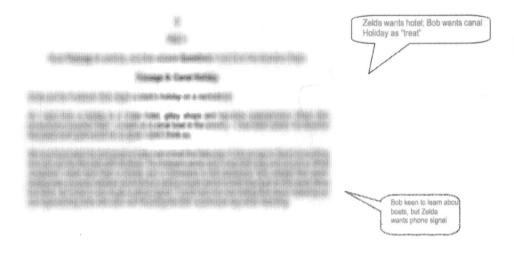

**DO: Now you make marginal markers in the rest of Passage A from the insert.**

After you've read Passage A and gone back through making marginal markers, set Passage A aside where you can't see it anymore.

3 **DO: In your notebook without Passage A in front of you, summarise the whole of Passage A in one or two sentences.**

After you have done this, then you can look at my example in the answers.[2]

*•Important Tip: You won't believe how many mistakes would be avoided in exams if students just get these basic facts right — that is, what the story is actually saying. By jotting your narration notes in the margin ("marginal markers"), you will benefit in two ways:*

   *•Cutting down on exam panic*

   *•Getting key details right*

DON'T PANIC: NARRATE FIRST

After all it IS a **reading** exam!

### ###

In Lesson One, you've learned:

•The CIE iGCSE exam comes in two parts:

  •Paper 0500-22 is the reading paper

  •Paper 0500-31 is the writing paper

•Reading and understanding the question is as important as reading/understanding the unseen passage

•Narrating your unseen passages by using marginal markers will help you understand the unseen passage before you start writing about it, and calm you down.

### ###

# Revision Suggestions from Lesson One: Copywork

1.Copywork is the easiest, most organic way to learn vocabulary, spelling, sentence construction, and all things connected to good writing.

2.You need good vocabulary, spelling, sentence structure, etc, for the CIE iGCSE English exams.

3.Therefore, you need to start doing copywork.

Basically, copywork is to writing what the "still life" is to painting — the basic building-block that all experts begin with before moving to better things.

In practical terms, you choose a very well-written book, and copy passages from it. Little and often is what's important.

For this course, you should do copywork

every day, taking just ten minutes for the task.

*Final assignment for Lesson One:*

*In your notebook, narrate what you learned in Lesson One. Remember, narration is a <u>closed book</u> skill, so don't review the lesson or refer back to the book. This is about strengthening your reading memory, so if you cheat and look, you're only making it harder to get ready for the exam.*

# Answers

1. The passage is told from the point of view of Zelda who is going on a canal boat holiday with her husband, Bob. She clearly isn't impressed by the idea of communing with nature or anything like that, because she keeps trying to get a phone signal instead of listening to instructions for driving the canal boat down the river, and clearly says she would prefer a 5-star holiday and pampering spa-type options than "a tube with windows." Bob, on the other hand, seems ultra-keen.

2. Bob takes Zelda on a canal-boat holiday, but she likes posh and civilised so complains all the time.

# LESSON TWO

In this lesson, we're going to turn our attention to Question 1 on the "Reading" paper, or 0500-21/22/23. We will be referring to the June 0500-22 paper, so you need to have it in front of you during this lesson.

First, let's review what we did in Lesson One.

> •We looked at the overview of the exam. It's delivered in two parts: 0500-22 (the reading paper) and 0500-31 (the writing paper).
>
> •We looked at 0500-22 and discovered it consists of 2 unseen passages and three questions, all of which are meant to be answered.
>
> •We learned a memory passage which is to be copied every day, we learned

about narration and writing marginal markers, and we had our first exposure to Passage A.

•You were assigned the task of writing marginal markers for Passage A (and getting the habit of doing this for all revision, whatever the subject), copying the memory verse, and starting daily copywork

## 0500-21/22/23 Question One at a Glance

Passage A in the insert has two corresponding questions for it in the question paper, Question 1 and Question 2.

Today, we are focusing on Question 1. To get a feel for the kind of question it is, refer to your copy of 0500-22 right now.

**DO: Read through the question on Page 2 of the question paper 0500-22. In your notebook, jot down your first**

**impressions of what it seems to want, how hard it might be, what you might want to include or leave out. These notes don't have to be in complete sentences.**

It's at this stage in the exam when you need your memory passage the most: that is, when reading the question. What is the memory passage? Say it out loud to yourself: if you don't remember it yet, look it up and read it out loud. _Don't skip this step: it's important._

**_Here are some of my observations about this question:_**

1.There are three parts to the answer,

bullet points which I will call A1, A2, and A3, because that's how the examiner will notate them when marking your answer;

2.The form, style, voice, and tone of it is that of a letter to a brother.

> •*Important Tip: There's no need to get over-zealous about this! It's just a "construct" to get you to change your viewpoint from Zelda to Bob, and to pick out details from the passage from his eyes, so remember the main point is to show off your reading skills, not chat with your brother about how his wife is doing or other irrelevancies. That just wastes precious time!*

3.Use your own words (don't copy phrases)

**DO: On your copy of the question paper, circle or underline the instructions that correspond to my observations 1, 2, and 3 above.**

Let's look at these 3 observations more closely.

1. There are three parts to the answer:

    •A1 = your expectations before the trip

    •A2 = your feelings about Zelda's behaviour

    •A3 = what happened the rest of the trip; these details are NOT in Passage A, but there are CLUES in the passage that you should use when writing this section

# A1

**DO: Look at the first two paragraphs of Passage A and see if you can pick out any details for the A1 portion of the answer, that is, what Bob was expecting from the trip. Write these down in your notebook.**

From the first paragraph, you might have picked up that Bob intended the trip to be a "treat", that it would offer peace and quiet, and maybe the suggestion that it's in the country might make you think that it's a break from the city.

From the second paragraph, you might have noted that Bob thought the pastime was "popular" so you could infer he thought he'd see people, that it would be a sociable holiday; the way he's so attentive to boat lingo might suggest to you that he expects to learn a new skill, that it's educational.

**DO: Look over my suggestions again and circle the key words in Passage A that link to my ideas. Notice how I take the surface meaning of Zelda's words and "read between the lines", picking up that Bob has heard about the popularity of boating and, by extension, would be expecting to meet people during the trip. This is a higher level of reading than simply identifying the reference to "peace" and "quiet" in paragraph one.**

—22·2·18

## A2

Now it's time to move onto A2. This is more tricky because Passage A is written from Zelda' viewpoint, but your answer has to be from Bob's. You will have to work hard to **infer** what Bob felt about Zelda's behaviour. This is a two-stage process. First, what did Zelda do, and second, what might Bob feel about that action.

In Passage A, look at the paragraph that begins "All this took too long."

5 **DO: Write a short narration of what Bob does in this paragraph. Then write what Zelda does. What do you think Bob might have felt about what Zelda did?**

To my mind, this paragraph is one where Bob is really "getting into" the whole boating scene. He isn't just listening patiently to the old gentleman as he rabbits on about boating; Bob is actually "plying" him with questions, meaning asking again and again for further information. Bob is really keen on this whole thing.

And Zelda? She is unhappy about the smelly boatyard and the thought of staying the night there, but Bob doesn't know these things because he's paying attention to the boatman, and Zelda is just thinking these things. The only thing that he could perhaps really know is that Zelda suddenly says she wants to go. What does that action suggest to him about her attitude?

I think there are two main ways you can read into Zelda's behaviour if you're Bob, and it depends on the kind of "Bob" you're going to be.

For example, if you are Bob and really wanted to have this boat trip because you want to get away from city life, a bit back to nature, enjoy a new hobby, and all the kinds of expectations we were looking at in A1, and Zelda suddenly seems bored, fed up, impatient to leave the boatyard where you had been fascinated by the boatman, how would you feel?

Probably equally fed up and annoyed. Zelda isn't "getting into the spirit" of it. She doesn't even seem to be *trying* to get into the spirit of it. She's letting you know that this was NOT her idea of a holiday, and she's probably trying to ruin it for you.

If you were Bob, you'd feel like anyone who was enthusiastic about something but who couldn't get your friend, your bae, your mum or dad keen about your hobby.

(Have you ever seen "Despicable Me"? Remember when Gru keeps trying to get his mother to acknowledge his brilliant inventions, and all she says is, "Meh." The response is really unsupportive, hurtful, and disheartening, isn't it?)

One possible answer: In this Bob persona, you could write to your brother: "I just really didn't understand Zelda's attitude. Here we were getting all this great information from the boatman about lingo and the area, and all she wanted to do was leave. I found it really frustrating."

That's Bob Mach 1.

What if, however, you were hen-pecked Bob. We'll call him Bob Mach 2. You feel guilty about bringing Zelda on the trip. You know she likes glitz and theatre and shopping, but you kind of hoped she'd enjoy herself once she got into the great outdoors, but now, you see you were wrong. You feel BAD! You want to be apologetic about the whole thing, and perhaps a bit of a limp dishrag about it.

**DO: Rewrite my answer above as an apologetic Bob, justifying Zelda's behaviour rather than being annoyed by it. Don't forget to express your feelings about her actions.**[1]

*•Important Tip: Note that the bullet point says write about YOUR FEELINGS (as Bob) about Zelda's behaviour, not just list what Zelda's behaviour was. There were a lot of students who struggled with the nuance of the question because they didn't read it carefully! (Memory Verse!!!!)*

A3

Finally, let's look at the third bullet point, A3. In this section, you are to *make up* or *create* things that you and Zelda did on the rest of the trip that aren't mentioned in Passage A.

However, don't think you can list a bunch of random things that aren't prepared for in the Passage. For example, you won't gain many points for saying you went bowling, sky-diving, or even gardening. You need to look carefully at the passage at ideas that were *planted* in it, natural progressions from what is already there.

Remember when I said earlier that Bob's expectations might include socialising with other boaters? Why not have them meet up with some other boaters?

**DO: Look carefully at Passage A and find some other people they could meet up with or do something with as an**

example of what they did on the rest of their trip. Circle the reference to them in the passage, and then in your notebook, jot down what Bob and Zelda did with them.

In the footnote, you'll see some of the people whom I think Bob and Zelda could have done something with, but of course, meeting people is just one activity that's planted in Passage A.[2]

- Can you find something about another restaurant to visit?
- Can you find something about a historical place to visit?
- Can you find something about nature study they could have done?

46

How do you think Zelda feels about these different activities? It's up to you to decide if she ever gets in the swing of things, if she continues to be a grump, or if, after all that trouble, Bob ends up calling off the whole trip and going home early.

General Point about Question 1

I hope you're getting the idea that reading the passage is sort of like a hunt for clues. Sure, there are easy, surface answers for the having, but anyone can find those. If it's easy enough that anyone can find them, you know they're not going to be useful for separating great answers from the MEHHHH ones.

So don't just read: read SMART!

Variations of Question 1:

Be aware that this question is only one type of question you might get.

This one, for example, is based on a passage with two characters, one of which is a viewpoint character. It's Zelda's version of the situation first, and you have to alter this viewpoint to be Bob's instead, and write his view in a different genre. While this approach is fairly typical, there are others that might crop up.

Another version you can get is a single person's specific story that needs to make use of that specific information and generalise it, usually to a different audience in a different genre: a story about someone's first horseback riding, say, turned into a speech about how one might ride a horse for the first time.

You can also get a story where the main character either has to write a journal entry about what happened in the story or where the character is interviewed by somebody:

this could be a manager asking what went wrong, or someone on the radio asking questions.

## The Bigger Point

In other words, practising past papers a lot is a good idea to see the different variations of this question, but it will never prepare you for ever option that might come up. That's why you need to be good at the SKILLS they're testing here:

- Can you read and understand what Passage A means on the surface?
- Can you read between the lines and infer information?
- Can you adopt a different viewpoint from the one in the passage?
- Can you alter the genre of passage to one with different audience, style, and purpose?

*Important Tip: Online, scripts are marked for three levels of reading for Question 1:*

   *•1.1) The <u>straightforward point,</u> say for example that Bob expected to treat Zelda with a canal boat holiday. Because this observations belongs to the first bullet point of the question, it would be labeled with an "A1". If, on the other hand, you were referring to the third bullet point, that Bob and Zelda met the celebrity couple and had drinks on their boat, then that would be noted by "A3". The more A1, A2, A3 you have, the higher your mark is likely to be.*

   *•1.2) Next comes the detail from the passage – he wanted "peace and quiet". These get tick marks*

*to show you referred to the insert. The more of these details, the higher your mark is likely to be.*

*•1.3) Finally, the development (DEV)... this is the "because" statement, such as Bob expected to have some peace and quiet on the holiday because they could get a change of scenery from the city, where it's implied they live.*

## Reading Ability is Important but Writing Ability Counts Too!

There are five marks available for your writing on this question, and this includes

•being able to use your own words and consider the audience appropriately;

•good sentence structures and variation;

•wide variety of vocabulary, accurate

spelling, competent punctuation;

•and organising your answer (using the bullet points as given in the question is the best idea).

BUT IT IS ONLY 5 POINTS!

In other words, don't sweat the details of the genre.

Yes, write a letter that starts: "Dear Brian, We've just come back from a trip I arranged for Zelda as a surprise" because that's what you've been told to do on the exam paper. However, it isn't helpful for your mark to expand this letter into too much chit-chat about your brother's life, his family, the swimming competitions they're doing, etc. This isn't a REAL letter: it's an exam answer, and it's testing how well you can pick out information, read between the lines, and develop your answer in good writing skills.

### ###

In Lesson Two, you've learned:

•Question 1 wants you to read Passage A and change the kind of writing it is and/or its viewpoint.

•Question 1 gives you a starting point that you should use, and three bullet points that you should follow.

•The more answers you find, details you include, and development you do, the better your mark is likely to be.

•There are also 5 points for writing that includes a lot of different skills.

•Remember that this is an exam answer that mainly shows off your reading ability, and doesn't really want you to "get into" the genre of the assignment so much that you forget to focus on the details of Passage A.

## Revision Suggestions from Lesson Two: Genres

## Review different kinds of writing

Here's a cheeky tip – go on-line to the book below, then choose the "look inside" option. Click through the various headings under Chapter 3 (writing skills), you will be able to easily review many of the conventions for writing on the exam.

You could even use "Print Screen" on your computer to capture the screen image print it out for studying.

On Amazon.co.uk, the book has been updated and has the cover on the left, but when you click "look inside" the book on the right comes up.

http://www.amazon.co.uk/Collins-Cambridge-IGCSE-English-Student/dp/000751705X/

### # # #

*Final assignment for Lesson Two:*

*DO: Try your hand at doing Question 1 on your own, following the tips and suggestions in this lesson. Then compare your answers to the mark scheme that's available to download online. How many of their expected points did you find?*

# Answers

1. The answer is your own choice, of course, but you could write something along the lines of: "I felt really bad for Zelda. I was listening to the boatman just yak and yak, and didn't even notice that Zelda was so tired. She had been working really hard, so when she wanted to leave suddenly, it just dawned on me about how selfish I was."

2. Some of the people I'd have Bob and Zelda meet would be the celebrity couple who have a boat on the canal; or, I'd have them try fishing; or, I'd have them go to the artists studio and meet the artist; or, I'd have them run into the chap with the dogs again, perhaps with better results this time.

# LESSON THREE

In this lesson, we're going to turn our attention to Question 2 on the "Reading" paper, or 0500-21/22/23. We will be referring to the June 0500-22 paper, so you need to have it in front of you during this lesson.

First. let's review what we did in Lesson Two.

- We looked at the advantage of using marginal markers on Passage A for calming down, for getting your facts right, and for making your comprehension stronger.
- We looked at Question 1 and thought about general principles –
  - Know your material before you start writing (narrate to solidify details)

57

- Know the style of writing required (report, letter, speech, interview, etc)
- Read the question carefully so you know what's important (make use of any bullet-point guidance)
- Don't lose sight of the point of the answer (which is to show that you have read carefully and accurately)

- We looked at the specifics of Question 1 on the 0500-22 from Jun 2015, and discovered that it wanted an answer in three parts, written as a friendly letter to a brother.

- We looked at how an answer like this is marked: addressing the bullet point (A1, A2, A3), detail from passage, and development ("because").

- For revision tips, your were

encouraged to look at a book that can help you learn more about different styles of writing, such as letters.

## 0500-21/22/23 Question Two at a Glance

This question is all about language analysis, and in my opinion, students really struggle with this. I am going to reveal to you the formula you can use to not only answer this question well, answer it easily, and answer it thoroughly, I believe you will also learn how to analyse literature effectively in general and — above all — finally understand what it's all about.

First, let's establish what Question 2 wants:

**•Can you choose words or phrases that add to the passage's meaning;**
**•Can you understand the basic meaning of the phrase you've chosen;**

**•Can you see how the author has used language to achieve certain effects?**

Therefore, you need to:

a) make good choices

b) explain the basic meaning (narration!)

c) explain how the author achieves effects.

***To me, effective language analysis is like peeling back the layers of an onion:***

Courtesy of Pixabay

I've created a five-step approach that I have called the HOW hand for helping you peel these layers in a focused and effective way.

I've called it the HOW hand because I use all five fingers of your hand to help you remember the five important steps. When you hold your hand with the palm out, as in a greeting to someone, it reminds me of the way that native Americans were stereotypically said to greet the white man in old cowboy film. Hand palm out, saying, "How!"

Edward S Curtis 1907

In list-form, this is how your five stages look:

1.Pick a good phrase or word

2.Pick ONLY a phrase or word, not a long sentence

3.Explain what it means in plain terms (the outer-most layer, or "just the facts, Ma'am")

4.Explain what else it can mean, or what it can suggest, or imply (a deeper layer of meaning)

5.Explain HOW the writer achieves effects by using this language

In visual form, it's like this:

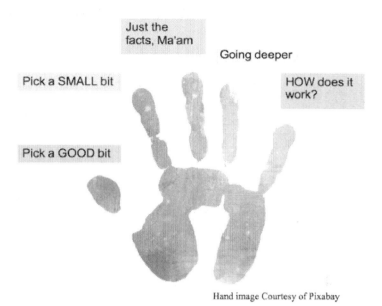

Just the facts, Ma'am

Going deeper

Pick a SMALL bit

HOW does it work?

Pick a GOOD bit

Hand image Courtesy of Pixabay

It's important to notice that your thumb and forefinger are about good choices — a crucial stage of this question. If you hold up just your thumb, it's like saying "good". If you hold your thumb and forefinger like a pretend gun-shape, then hopefully, you can think of this stage as pointing at a target. You want to hit the bulls-eye.

The other three fingers are the steps toward

deepening the layers of your explanation.

<u>A challenging example</u>

Below, I have copied a passage from Mary Shelley's <u>Frankenstein</u>, a book I teach in my online literature classes.

In this scene, the main character, Victor has run away to the mountains where he gathers strength from being in nature. (In actual fact, this scene is a flashback, but that doesn't really matter in our analysis of the language in it)

> Presently a breeze dissipated the cloud, and I descended upon the glacier. The surface is very uneven, rising like the <u>waves of a troubled sea</u>, descending low, and interspersed by rifts that sink deep. The <u>field of ice is</u> almost a league in width, but I spent nearly two hours in crossing it. The

opposite      mountain      is      a      bare
perpendicular rock.

**DO: Can you see any words or phrases
that stick out as especially literary or
notable? Jot them down in your
notebook before I tell you a couple I've
picked out as possibilities.**

Basically, this passage is full of a lot of big
words, but most of them are just big-word
ways of describing the scene. In my own
words, my narration would go something
like this: the wind blew the clouds away to
make a blue sky, and Victor climbed the
glacier, which was undulating up and down
and, occasionally, had a big, deep crack in

65

it. It was icy and a far distance (League = 3 miles, but you didn't really need to know that), and Victor didn't cross it very quickly. Where he was headed was a massive mountain, jutting up to the sky directly in front of him without any grass, trees, or other vegetation.

However, amongst all those words that were merely description, and therefore, not particularly interesting to analyse, there was an example of a common literary device. Did you find it?

It was the simile "rising like the waves of a troubled sea". Similes are almost always good choices to pounce on in a passage, because they are deliberately literary, and often, add to the picture — or image — in your head. Your job now is to explain what kind of image is in your head because of it.

However, most students fall down right

here. Instead of explaining what the phrase means, they simply label it as a simile and think they're done. If you look at the CIE mark scheme, this is almost always described as "correctly identify linguistic devices but not explain why they are used," and comes from a lower tier mark called Band 4.

## YOU CAN DO BETTER THAN THAT!!!

Here's how we unpack this simile, using the HOW hand.

> Presently a breeze dissipated the cloud, and I descended upon the glacier. The surface is very uneven, rising like the waves of a troubled sea, descending low, and interspersed by rifts that sink deep. The field of ice is almost a league in width, but I spent nearly two hours in crossing it. The opposite mountain is a bare

perpendicular rock.

First, we write down our good bit/small bit:

rising like the waves of a troubled sea

Our next step is just re-telling back what it means in our own words. In other words, the surface meaning, or what I like to call "just the facts, ma'am" — I've named it after an old cop show in the US called Dragnet where one of the detectives wouldn't let any witnesses embellish their version of events. He only wanted the facts. Just the facts. (You can Google YouTube to find some old episodes. There's a clip to the 1987 film re-make with Dan Akroyd and Tom Hanks on metacafe, but the suggested links after are very dodgy, so I haven't included the link here!)

So, that's why I call the third step "just the facts, ma'am." You need to hone down the meaning of the phrase before you go explaining the simile or anything else. Here is an example of "Just the facts, ma'am&rdquo to go along with our Frankenstein good bit/small bit:

**Victor is describing the surface of the glacier where he's walking, and it's not smooth.**

> •*Important Tip: You have now made a good choice (step 1 and step 2: good bit/small bit), and have explained what it means on the surface (step 3: just the facts, ma'am). Even if you just do this for every selection on Question 2, you have successfully identified meanings, and this falls in the mark scheme as Band 3.*

The next step — step 4 on our HOW hand — is "going deeper". Here is where you can make connections, widen the idea, make a bridge between what the phrase means on its surface, and step 5 which will be the literary bit.

In our example here, it might be something along the lines of:

**In fact, the surface seems to resemble the waves of a stormy ocean, that is, very up-and-down as opposed to gentle ripples.**

This is already a pretty good answer to this point, but to hit the "home run", so to speak, you have to explain HOW the author is creating an effect with word choices here, especially in terms of widening the understanding of the reader.

•*Important Tip: The key to a great Question 2 is this final step. Think about these words for a minute. Why would Shelley want to compare the glacier to an ocean? PLEASE don't say "because it makes it stand out more". Blech, blech, blech. She would make it "stand out more" if she compared it to an ice rink, a mud pit, a marshmallow. The point is, she compared it to a stormy sea, so I ask you again, what does this SPECIFIC comparison DO???*

Picture it. I mean, really try to picture a stormy sea. What does it look like? Now transpose that idea onto a sheet of ice. What does that make the ice look like?

It's all up-and-down, higgledy-piggledy, churned up. Peaks and troughs. There's nothing calm about these scenery. Instead, you could argue that it's rather dangerous, like a stormy sea is to a ship, for example.

Therefore, for my fifth and final step of the HOW hand, I might write something like this:

**Using the words "troubled sea" to describe the ice, Shelley suggests that the scenery isn't a place of peace and quiet, as perhaps Victor had hoped, but instead, somewhere that's stormy, uncertain, perhaps even dangerous.**

Can you see how I have fully explained what that simile is doing there, not just saying that "it sticks out", but that it gives an additional feeling of disquietude where otherwise you might expect peace.

*Here's how to write out your answer:*

"rising like the waves of a troubled sea"

(In this phrase, the author is describing the surface of the glacier where Victor is walking, and it's not smooth) (In fact, the surface seems to resemble the waves of a stormy ocean, that is, very up-and-down.) (Using the words "troubled sea" to describe the ice, Shelley suggests that the scenery isn't a place of peace and quiet, as perhaps Victor had hoped, but instead, somewhere that's stormy, uncertain, perhaps even dangerous.)

•*Important Tip: Since this question does not mark your writing ability, but only your analytical understanding, you don't have to worry about essay form. In fact, it's much simpler and easier to simply write an answer as I've done above.*

NOTE: Although I am giving you a formula for tackling language analysis — a step-by-step process so you leave no stone unturned in this exam — please don't disengage your thinking muscles! THINK THINK THINK.

Consider the WHOLE context of what surrounds your good bit, small bit; otherwise, you analyse one little phrase, forget the rest of the sentence it comes from, and say the STUPIDEST things.

For example, if you take "like a troubled sea" out of the context of the glacier where Victor is walking, you miss the point that it's ice in the Alps, and might just focus on a churning ocean all by itself. If you do that, you miss the contrast between what he expected by going to the mountains (snowy swathes of comforting white), and what he actually got (jaggedy, up-and-down ice).

**DO: Use five different-coloured pens or pencils, and underline the parts in "Here's how to write out your answer" above that correspond to**

•good bit
•small bit

(•just the facts, ma'am )

(•going deeper )

( •HOW does it work)

Yes, the first two are the same phrase, but I still want you to underline it in two different colours so you come to understand that they're each important, even though (when you get it right) they refer to the same choice of text.

## SUMMARY ABOUT QUESTION 2

*Analysing language is a) about good choices, and b) about telling both meaning and effect, and c) thinking around the phrase so you don't analyse in isolation and say something that shows you didn't read very carefully after all!*

Question 2 from 0500-22

Now it's time to refer to your question paper and get some practice at HOW hand for yourself. The instructions on the exam for Question 2 will tell you which two paragraphs you're to focus on; it's no good picking out interesting words and phrases from any other part of Passage A than the one the exam tells you to look at (remember your memory verse???).

In this case, your task is to look at two specific paragraphs and:

> •find "powerful" words and phrases from each of these paragraphs (that would be the "good bit" from our HOW hand);

> •include imagery (in other words, word

pictures);

•explain HOW the choice is used effectively.

Let's start with Paragraph 6 from the insert, which starts: "No sooner were we inside." The task says to look at words and phrases about the storm and its effects.

**DO: Read through Paragraph 6 and pick a good bit/small bit. Start by choosing the obvious and easy phrases first, such as similes. Once you have picked the obviously literary simile, write out your "just the facts, ma'am" where you tell back in plain terms exactly what that phrase is talking about in the context of the story.**

The only simile in this paragraphs is the one in the first sentence, "like machine gun fire." If you were to write the just the facts, ma'am, of JUST this little phrase, you might say something like "it sounded like a machine gun going off." However, you need a bit more than this to properly explain what that simile means — WHAT sounds like machine gun fire? The rain! More specifically, Zelda thought the rain from the storm sounded like machine gun fire as it pelted the roof of the boat.

BUT WAIT!!!! It's really important that you put "just the facts, ma'am," into your own words. The reason is this — many students who are not native English speakers or who are not very strong in English will simply parrot back a phrase when they don't really understand what it means, so the mark scheme is very clear in expecting that good answers will not "repeat the language of the original."

Try instead something like this:

The rain on the canal boat's roof sounded like the rapid, heavy pattering of shots from an automatic gun.

*(Note: Occasionally, you might feel the need to undertake massive verbal gymnastics in order to avoid the original language; if you think it's getting a bit silly — I mean, how else can you say a "dog" unless you twist yourself in all kinds of unnecessary knots — then in that case, it's probably ok to use the original word. Just make sure that you include enough detail that the examiner can tell you really understand what you're talking about)*

Next, Step Four in the HOW hand wants you do "go further". This step is in here so you don't leap to literary labelling and, thus, don't explain how your thought processes got there.

This is just like my earlier example of Victor on the glacier. Shelley went against expectations of a smooth, peaceful ice rink, and connected the scenery to a stormy ocean.

In the exam's Passage A, the good bit/small bit is taking the topic of rain and relating it to an instrument of warfare.

**DO: Think about the connection between rain and machine guns. Describe in your own words what machine-gun rain would sound like, and the kind of feeling it's creating for the scene. Check my suggestions below once you've jotted down your thoughts.** [1]

So far, you have chosen a good bit/small bit. You have written a sentence of just the facts, ma'am. Now you have added the going further, explaining the transition of rain into something loud, rapid, and probably, quite violent or aggressive.

What do you think the author is trying to tell us about this rain storm by making this simile? Clearly, it's not meant to be your usual pitter-patter experience! No comparisons to playful kittens, in other words!

To help you, we're going to play multiple choice quiz. From the following options, which "HOW" explanation is closest to what the simile is doing here:

A.By comparing the rain to a machine gun, the author is making it all stand out.

B.By comparing the rain to a machine gun, the author is talking about how loud the rain is.

C.By comparing the rain to a machine gun, the author is suggesting that this is an aggressive and violent storm.

D.By comparing the rain to a machine gun, the author uses a simile that describes the storm.

Hopefully, you chose the right answer. You can check in the answer section.[2]

**DO: Go back over this sub-section and find my example of the five HOW had steps, writing them down in the same form as I did for the Frankenstein example. Compare your version to my answer.[3]**

## About Overview

One final touch you can put on your responses to Question 2 is that of "overview", where you consider several of these good bit/small bit answers as a group, or look at the paragraph as a whole.

For example, if you look back over Paragraph 6, what would you say is the overall feel for weather? Even just a glance at some of the key words — hammering, shrieking, snatched — point to a rather frightening, noisy, and powerful storm.

**DO: Re-read Paragraph 7 now that begins "Having only managed ...". What is the overall feel for this paragraph?**

# What are some of the key words that made you say this?[4]

•*Important Tip: Choices on Question 2 are really key. The mark scheme dictates which choices are considered acceptable. In other words, if you thought a good bit from Paragraph 6 was "the wind rose" or "the boat pitched at its mooring", then you would be out of luck. They don't appear on the mark scheme, and you would actually be penalised for making poor choices.*

### ###

In Lesson Three, you've learned:

•Make sure you know which paragraphs you are to take words and phrases from in Passage A.

•Make sure you pick out words/phrases that have layers of meaning/ anything with obvious literary techniques like metaphors, personification, etc, are good to choose. It shows you understand how techniques work.

•Don't quote too long a section; a few words at most; otherwise, you don't get credit for more than one accepted item in the phrase.

•Choose quality over quantity in terms of how many phrases you write about – the minimum should be 3 from each paragraph if you write the length of my example, plus some overview if you have time.

•Use your HOW hand to write a complete answer - the outer layer, the inner layer, and the techniques used — don't just label; explain!

###

# Revision Suggestions from Lesson Three: Genres

## Review Literary Terms

It's really important for Question 2 that you know literary terms and how they work. Otherwise, you haven't got the knowledge to know what makes a good phrase, and you haven't got the vocabulary or understanding to explain HOW the author achieves effects with that phrase.

Since these are the two objectives being examined in Question 2, you need to know literary terms!

There are several pages of literary terms with brief explanations of HOW they work at this BBC Bitesizelink:

http://www.bbc.co.uk/education/guides/zs9g tyc/revision

However, no need to go "overboard" with all the different techniques: those on their first page will probably do — simile, metaphor, onomatopoeia, alliteration, personification.

*Final assignment for Lesson Three:*

*DO: Find as many past papers for Paper 2 and print off their Passage A, their question 2 from the question paper, and their mark scheme for question 2. Remember that this question hasn't changed for years, so you can easily go back 5 years or more, and print off Winter and Summer exams, all three versions. Then with a partner or a parent, see how many of the good bit/small bit choices you can make that are included as official answers in the mark scheme.*

# Answers

1. Really heavy rain like this is usually the result of a storm, and suggests really violent, intense amounts of water pouring down. Added to that the idea of "machine gun", this is a violent and aggressive, even dangerous storm.

2. C

3. like machine gun fire.
The rain on the canal boat's roof sounded like the rapid, heavy pattering of shots from an automatic gun. The rain is loud and intense, part of a bad storm. By comparing the rain to a machine gun, the author is suggesting that this is an aggressive and violent storm.

4. You might have found the smiling sun, the

feathery clouds, the pale blue sky, and the little pearl-like droplets of water, and from these clues, deduced a calm, gentle, friendly, peaceful kind of morning.

# LESSON FOUR

In this lesson, we're going to turn our attention to Question 3 on the "Reading" paper, or 0500-21/22/23. We will be referring to the June 0500-22 paper, so you need to have it in front of you during this lesson.

First. let's review what we did in Lesson Three.

> •We were exposed to the HOW hand and its five steps to successful literary analysis.
>
> •We looked at Question 2 and that it wanted to find out:
>
> > •Can you choose words or phrases that create deeper meaning;
> >
> > •Can you understand the basic meaning of the phrase you've chosen;

•Can you see how the author has used language to achieve certain effects?

•For revision tips, your were encouraged to look at some online resources for strengthening your knowledge of literary terms.

0500-21/22/23 Question Three at a Glance

The one about pinpoint comprehension and turning a list into a summary

Question 3 comes in two parts:

3a) you write a list of fifteen points which you pick out from Passage B from the exam's insert;

3b) you take these same fifteen points and write them in sentences, using your own words.

It should be an easy question — just read a passage and write down fifteen relevant points. However, it seems to give a lot of students problems. Do they make it too hard? Do they over-think it? Are they just too freaked out and scared?

I'm not sure what it is for individuals, but in general, the biggest mistake is:

## Students don't read the question!

This is one reason that I have you copy down that memory verse every day as part of your revision. Honestly, if you can't read the question properly, then how can you give the correct answer? It's just logic!

Other mistakes that students make are:

•1.1 They don't think about some answers being examples of the same point

•1.2 They can't limit themselves to 15 good examples

•1.3 They insist on writing intros and conclusions in 3b

Here are some tips for approaching Question 3 in a systematic and focused way.

•Make sure you read the question

•With the task in mind, first go through the passage and underline points that you think are relevant

•Briefly evaluate the points in light of the question, and group those that are versions of the same point

•Write down your fifteen points. You cannot write more than fifteen, and if you try to put more than one point on any line, only one will be counted.

•You can just copy the words from the passage exactly in 3a, and don't need to paraphrase in your own words.

Sometimes, students get into problems because they write such short notes that their answers aren't clear. For example, if the question wanted to know what a detective saw on his travels, then you could choose from a hypothetical passage the word "buildings". Probably in your head, this is not very detailed, but it may be more or less true. However, if the sentence in the insert actually said "abandoned buildings", then you would do better to write the bigger phrase "abandoned buildings" than just a single word "buildings".

We'll look at this more in a minute with your specific example so that my tip makes more sense.

Question 3a from 0500-22

Now it's time to refer to your question paper and Passage B from the insert, and get some practice with your pinpoint accuracy and your dense summaries.

First, let's look at the instructions from the question paper. While looking at it, underline the following points on it:

•a) write in short notes

•b) you do not need to use your own words

•c) the question is about *challenges faced during the construction* of the Panama Canal. Note that it's NOT asking about the history of the canal, how the canal works, or details about, for example, the lake along the way. Underline this phrase to remind you what you're looking for as you read Passage B.

Finally, just before you start reading Passage B and finding answers in it, locate the italicised description of what Passage B is about. Underline it to give you context for the piece you're about to read.

Answering strategy:

Now, just read a sentence at a time from Passage B. After each sentence, ask yourself: is this about the challenges faced when constructing the canal? If it isn't, just move on.

**DO: Using a pen/pencil, go through the first three paragraphs of Passage B and underline phrases that mention problems that were faced when building the canal.**[1]

*•Important Tip: There are two issues to keep in the back of your mind as you pick out the relevant phrases you want*

*to write in your fifteen lines.*

*•First, combining similar issues. It's important to realise that Question 3a isn't about finding the first fifteen points you come to in Passage B. Some of the answers are different ways of saying the same thing, so for example, you might be tempted to write that it was costly, a company went bankrupt, and an American company spent $387 million, thinking that these were worth three points, but actually, all three points are grouped under the subject of expense.*

*•Second, separating similar issues. Conversely, there are some exams where splitting topics is actually correct, especially if*

you're asked about the differences between two things. This is a bit of a vague point as I'm trying not to give away answers to any mocks you might take, but let's say you were asked to write an answer based on two vehicles, a petrol-based one and an electric one. Perhaps the question is written as such that you compare the differences between them, then it might be appropriate that one answer was that the fuel they used are separate points — petrol and electric — for 2 marks, and not the single mark for the generalised point about fuel. Be careful that the issues really are separate: if you wrote "One was bigger" on one line, and

*"One was smaller" on another line, then you've just said the same thing in two different ways.*

With these tips in mind, go back over your third paragraph and see if there are any challenges that could be combined. I'll do one to start with: malaria and yellow fever would be part of the same problem, which might be said to be health risks or diseases. If I were to answer this question, I would put malaria and yellow fever on the same line instead of on two different ones, and I would receive one mark for the two phrases.

**DO: Circle two points in the third paragraph that are connected with difficult terrain or problems with the geography of the area.**[2]

More Revision Practice Ideas:

Although this is a fairly new format for

0500, you would still benefit from going over past papers in the old form, just seeing if you can identify salient – that means "relevant" – points.

It will also help you practise past papers in terms of reading the question. I can't stress enough how many mistakes are made on 3a because students don't read the focus of the question carefully enough.

<u>Question 3b from 0500-22</u>

Question 3b is simply taking your 15 points from 3a, and turning them into a flowing passage of prose that you've written now in your own words.

The key word for this answer is:

That says "Dense". Meaning, you need to write in a very focused way.

Taking the seven points that we found in the third paragraph of the insert, and "wrote" into our answer for 3a, let's look at how I'd turn this into a dense summary for 3b.

*Some of the challenges faced by building the canal were engineering problems, bad living conditions for the workers, and difficulty in managing the project. There were a lot of illnesses like malaria because of the area, and mosquitos were contributing to health issues, so they required actions like spraying and draining the swamps. The land caused issues, too, like too much rain causing the mud to collapse back into the excavations, and these obstacles all mounted up in terms of the high cost of the project.*

You would go on in this vein with the rest of the eight points in the mark scheme from 3a, making sure that you stay focused, use your own words within reason, and aim for fluency.

But can you see the catch?

*We're not looking — maybe the catch will go away.*

The catch is that your fifteen choices from Question 3a have to be good, or your summary in 3b won't be concise, dense, and accurate.

<u>*Question 3b is looking for:*</u>

  *•Using your own words*
  *•Writing fluently*

•Packing in the points from 3a so that the summary is concise

•Avoiding introductions, conclusions, or unnecessarily long explanations

•Important Tip: There are two additional "boosts" to your answer that are available to you. First, is just having some nice writing — good vocabulary, strong sentences. The second is organising your answer, especially grouping ideas that were spread out in Passage B. Remember the grouping of ideas in 3a, where I mentioned that yellow fever and malaria were actually one point about health dangers. As these were dangers to people, you could group other topics together, such as diseases, housing, draining swamps, netting, and high death toll.

•That said, let's be realistic. This is only a 5-point question. If the difference between getting down all your answers in a concise way, and getting them successfully clumped on top of that, will gain you only a single point, then is it worth using those precious minutes for this purpose???

•It's a trade-off, so weight up advantages/disadvantages about this. The point of 3b is that it should be a quick in-and-out answer to grab a few extra points, not something to sweat and slave over when you need those precious minutes for your other answers.

•Finally: check the word limit. Dense and concise doesn't mean short!

---

# Here's a Crazy Idea!

What if you actually START on Question 3 in the exam? You could decide to use only ½ hour on it to grab a good dozen marks before turning your attention to questions 1 and 2.

Believe it or not, there's even an argument for doing the whole paper backwards. Think about it — Question 1 is the trickiest in terms of taking time over it, and you might gain insight for Question 1 by doing

Question 2 first. I mean, did you notice how Zelda's attitude on the morning after the storm was starting to soften toward her surroundings, finding the scenery inviting, quiet, and precious? Knowing that before writing Question 1 could have a big effect on the A3 section of your answer!

If you do decide to tackle the paper backwards, you must start doing this on all your mocks and practices!

### 

In Lesson Four, you've learned:

•Make sure you have read and understood the question. (memory verse!)

•Take all your answers from 3a and write them in your own words in fluent sentences for 3b.

•Your answer will be stronger if you can

group topics together rather than list them chronologically from the passage, but if you're running out of time, it's better to get 4 points than none!

•Your answer will also be strong if you:

> •don't write an intro or conclusion

> •don't waffle and explain too much, but just churn out those fifteen points.

•Consider starting with Question 3.

### ###

## Revision Suggestions from Lesson Four: Expose Yourself

### Explore a wide variety of genres

What I mean by "expose yourself" has nothing to do with macks and a lack of underwear! Instead, I mean it's time to intentionally gather, read, and study the kinds of writing that you might have to produce in your 0500 exams.

What kinds of writing might you have to do? According to CIE's spec, you could have to write:

- a report,
- a letter,
- a journal (like a diary),
- a speech,
- an interview,
- a newspaper report,

•or a magazine article.

Also, you will be reading inserts in your exams that may be taken from similar kinds of writing, so the more "exposure" you have to a variety of written materials, the better.

Start picking up a variety of papers and magazines from newsagents, look up Martin Luther King, Jr's "I have a dream" speech or Sojourner Truth's "Ain't I a woman" speech, google some reports, look up some extracts from Anne Frank's diary or other famous diary writers, find radio transcripts of interview ... I think you get the drift, right?

**DO: Print out the bullet-point list above and cross out each one as you deliberately revise the different kinds of writing.**

Finally, add another 5 minutes to your copywork every day, where you copy from an example from your "exposure" texts as well as your literary text.

All this being said, remember that genre conventions are only a portion of your mark. It's much more important to be able to understand the passages from the exam, so while you're "exposing yourself" to all these different genres, it would be equally important to narrate all of them to practise your comprehension.

Don't forget to challenge yourself sometimes with harder examples!

*Final assignment for Lesson Four:*

*DO: To help you get to grips with 3b, use the answers for 3a from 0500-22's mark scheme to write your most succinct and well-sequenced summary.*

*Choose only fifteen of the twenty suggested points. Make sure you write it by hand, unless you know you have permission to use a computer in the exam. After you've written your summary, then take a brightly-coloured marker and put a big tick on top of each of the points you've made from 3a. Are there lots of them, clumped together? Good. Did you write at least 180 words? Good. If not, you need to write more. Did you include an introductory sentence or conclusion that has no tick marks? Naughty, naughty! You're stuck at 4/5 at most. The last self-check stage is to let someone like your parent read the summary out loud and narrate back to you what they think you mean. The reason you do this is that sometimes you've been too general or described the 3a details inaccurately, and only by getting a fresh eye will you learn when you make this mistake.*

# Answers

1. When I did this exercise, I didn't find anything relevant to the question until the third paragraph, and then, I found 7 things.

2. The specific parts to circle would be the rain-induced mudslides and the steep angle. If you chose the "unstable mountain", that's actually a separate point to do with rock issues, more examples of which come later in Passage B.

# Lesson Five

In this lesson, we're going to turn our attention to the Writing Paper, or 0500-31/32/33. We will be referring to the June 0500-31 paper, so you need to have it in front of you during this lesson.

First. let's review what we did in Lesson Four.

- •We looked at Question 3 (in general) is trying to test:
    - •If you can pick out a large number of salient points
    - •If you can write them succinctly and densely
- •We looked at the list of choices in 3a and the summary in 3b.
- •We talked about how it's possible to re-order your approach to Paper 22 if

you wanted to start with Question 3.

•The revision tip of the day was about "exposure" — as in, exposing yourself to the types of writing you might have to produce for the exam: articles, reports, diaries, speeches, etc.

## 0500-31/32/33 in General

•Paper 3 is known as the "writing" paper for the iGCSE, but the first question still receives 10 out of 25 points for assessing your reading!

•Some of the important objectives for this paper are to:

  •order your thoughts,

  •demonstrate a range of vocabulary,

  •write appropriately for your intended audience,

  •and show accurate use of mechanics such as grammar,

punctuation, etc.

There are two fundamental tasks on this paper:

1. You must have a good grasp of audience and purpose for whichever question you answer;
2. You must aim to write fluidly, accurately, and in an orderly manner on all answers.

## The Key to the Writing Paper is:

HATS!

Yes, that's right: HATS.

Before you start doing any writing, you need

to think through the various kinds of writing styles, tones of voice, purposes, and audiences you're aiming to implement in your answers.

I think it's a bit like looking for a holiday cottage (stay with me — the analogy comes back to hats in a minute). When I look for a cottage, I go onto Google and first get about 50,000 hits for all the holiday cottages in Britain. So, I choose an area of the country to focus on, and that eliminates about 45,000 cottages.

Now I have 5,000 to choose from, but I have a big family. And a dog. So, I choose various "filters" to narrow my choices more.

By now, I have probably 30 choices — big cottages in the area I want that allow pets. Next filter is the dates I want to travel. Voila! I have successfully limited my choice to one or two, and now I start to contact the rental company and sort out my accommodation.

The hat analogy for the Writing Paper is like this. Rather than filtering out choices as I would do for a holiday home, you are going to figuratively pile hats on your head to achieve the right combination of styles, tones, and purposes for your exam answer.

For each question on the paper that you choose to answer, you will "pile" four hats on your head as part of your pre-writing phase. These hats come under the categories:

- Genre hats – what are the conventions of the type of writing? Letters vs speeches vs articles vs essays
- Audience hats – who are you writing for? Adults, children, friends, strangers, general?
- Writer hats – what kind of tone of

voice do you want to aim for (formal, informal; persuasive, angry, descriptive, analytical)

•Purpose hats – why are you writing? Inform, persuade, instruct?

Notice if you circle each of the first initials of these four hats, you get an acronym: GAWP. I know sometimes revision guides talk about only "GAP", but honestly, if you don't think about the kind of attitude and tone of the writer, you can miss the nuances of addressing your answer appropriately.

One way I like to remember this acronym GAWP is to think of someone actually GAWP-ing.

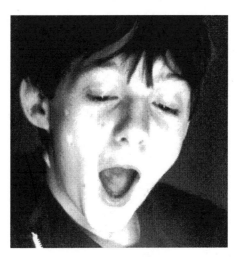

## To Gawp:

*An expression of surprise or alarm*
*OR*
*An acronym to help you write better for the exam*

G for Genre:

Your genre hats are the ones you choose from to decide the style of writing. A letter is different from a speech, is different from a newspaper article, is different from a journal entry.

A for Audience:

After reminding yourself the conventions for

the genre you're supposed to write in, think about who the audience is for the piece. Is it a colleague, a superior officer, a councillor, a teacher, a parent, and brother? Each of these would require a different approach, so be sure to put on your audience hat before you begin to write.

W for Writer:

The oft-overlooked hat. This one makes you think about the persona you're adopting. Are you writing with brother affection, the assertiveness of a concerned citizen, the defensiveness of someone who has made a mistake?

P for Purpose:

This is no-doubt a familiar decision when getting ready to write something — are you doing it to persuade, inform, entertain?

**DO: Practise some GAWP-ing right now**

by jotting down the GAWP of each of these scenarios:

1.A letter to a friend

2.An interview with your father about his time in the war

3.A letter of complaint to your local councillor about broken park equipment

4.A speech to other homeschooled kids about taking up sport

5.A newspaper article about the closure of a nearby recycling plant

6.An magazine article about keeping different kinds of pets

7.A report about use of swimming pools in your county

8.A journal entry about being grounded

The answers are in the footnotes.[1]

REMEMBER that GAWP is really GAWPe (you say this "gawp-ee"). Just like I said about Question 1 on the Reading Paper - where you're supposed to write a letter to your brother, but it's not like any REAL letter you'd write to your brother - you always have to have the fact that it's an exam you're writing.

So one of the hats you always wear is the "e" hat for "exam".

GAWP-e Hat

•Next time, we will look more carefully at mechanics, especially the difference between run-on sentences, and sentence fragments.

•Suffice to say, this is a more serious subject than most people realise, and often fail to give it the attention it needs.

•In this paper, for example, your mechanics make up about 1/3 of the points of Question 1, and nearly HALF the points for the Question 2.

•It is possible to underperform on this criterion alone.

•This is silly. You should know how to write, punctuate, spell, and manipulate your native language, especially in an exam that's about that very subject!

You still have time to do something about this!

•*Important Tip: Doing copywork routinely will help your spelling, punctuation, grammar, and vocabulary a lot more than any workbook or even endless correction of your written work.*

•*A free grammar workbook focusing on sentences can be found at the following link:* http://www.classiclanguagearts.ne t/lists/grammar-workbook/

•*It is a challenging 100-page document. I don't mean for you to go through all its exercises, but if you at least read its prose summaries at the beginning of each chapter, you'll get a good overview and some extra help.*

•*I believe you'll get the most out of it if your parents help you study it, especially guiding you to focus on those chapters where you have weaknesses.*

### #

In Lesson Five, you've learned...

## *A MAJOR PART OF THE 0500-31/32/33 PAPER IS ...*

### ... **HOW WELL YOU GAWP!**

•Think of it in terms of hats, piling them up before you start to write.

•Don't forget the fifth hat – "e" – the fact that you're taking an exam!

Next time, we will look at Question 1 and more                                    GAWP.

Plus, about structuring your answers, which is another big part of 0500-31/32/33. Plus, in our revision sections, we'll be talking about your writing "mechanics" or proficiency.

# Revision Suggestions from Lesson Five:
## Let's Eat Grandpa!*
## Mechanics Part A

Mechanics means your spelling, punctuation, grammar, sentence structures, etc.

Do you know what's wrong with the following sentences and phrases?

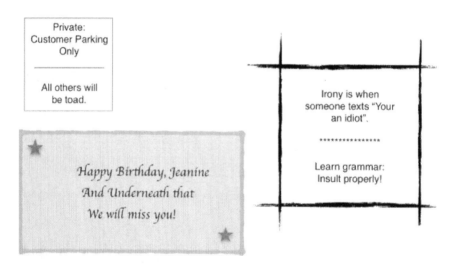

It's important to know correct vocabulary and correct punctuation — it might save a life!

**\*"Let's eat Grandpa" means that you're planning to dine on your grandad. Probably, the writer actually meant, "Let's eat, Grandpa," as in, "Come on, Grandpa, let's go get some food."**

Here's a link to 15 grammar goofs that make you look silly: http://www.copyblogger.com/grammar-goofs/

And another helpful website for grammar issues: http://www.bristol.ac.uk/arts/exercises/grammar/grammar_tutorial/index.htm

*Final assignment for Lesson Five:*

*DO: Refer to past papers and find at least one example of a journal, an article, an interview, a letter, a report, and a speech. Make a list of the GAWP of each one, paying particularly close*

*attention to how they differ from each other in the "G" category.*

# Answers

1. 1. letter, friend, friendly and chatty, inform and share perhaps persuade; 2. interview, father, interested and questioning, explore; 3. letter, local councillor, probably concerned or aggrieved (but not aggressive), probably persuasive; 4. speech, other homeschooled kids, probably like a big brother giving advice, persuasive; 5. newspaper article, local readership, objective, to inform; 6. magazine article, unspecified but maybe children/young adults/full-time workers, informed/expert, to inform; 7. a report, perhaps to the council/swim company/parents, informed and factual, to inform; 8. diary, to self, annoyed/perhaps humbled and sorry, to let off steam.

# LESSON SIX

In this lesson, we're going to turn our attention to Question 1 of 0500-31/32/33. We will be referring to the June 0500-31 paper, so you need to have it in front of you during this lesson.

First. let's review what we did in Lesson Five.

> •We saw that, though it's known as the "writing paper", there are still 10 marks out of 25 in Question 1 that assesses your ability to read carefully.
>
> •We saw that this paper is testing various objectives, including:
>
>> •ordering your thoughts,
>>
>> •demonstrating vocabulary,
>>
>> •writing appropriately for an audience,

•showing accurate use of mechanics.

•I told you that there were two fundamental tasks for the Writing Paper, which were:

> •You must have a good grasp of audience and purpose for whichever question you answer;

> •You must aim to write fluidly and accurately on all answers

•We then went on to look at the different kinds of "hats" that one needs to put on (metaphorically) in order to write appropriately for this exam.

*NOTE: choosing hats is also a good way of considering how to appropriately write ANYTHING in real life, too!*

> •There were four different hats to wear for almost any kind of writing: the acronym I chose for this is GAWP.

•Finally, we looked briefly at the importance of mechanics like grammar, punctuation, etc, and I encouraged you to revise these as much as the techniques of each exam question.

## 0500-31/32/33 Overview

**DO: Look at the cover page of the Question Paper in front of you. Find the paragraph that begins "Answer two questions in the space provided." With a bright-coloured pen or highlighter, underline or highlight where it says "two questions". Do the same for "Question 1 in Section 1, and the ONE question from Section 2." Also underline where it says that you need to clearly write the question number you choose from Section 2 at the start of your answer.**

Note also that there are a total of 50 points for this paper.

You MUST answer Question 1. It's similar to Question 1 of 0500-22 in that you have an insert that you need to read, make marginal markers on, then re-work the material into a different genre of writing. It needs more focus on GAWP than 0500-22 does.

Whereas Question 1 from 0500-22 is marked 15 points for reading and 5 for writing, in 0500-31, you are marked 15 points for writing and 10 points for reading. That's a total of 25 points on the Writing Paper, compared to only 20 points for the Reading paper.

Then, in Part 2, there is a CHOICE between four questions — 2 choices that are descriptive writing, and 2 choices that are narrative writing. You answer ONLY ONE of these, for a total of 25 points.

*NOTE — there used to be THREE kinds of writing in Part 2, but since Winter 2014, the option for a discursive essay has been removed. This doesn't mean that past papers prior to June 2015 are useless for revising, but it does mean that they will differ in this regard.*

The 25 points for Part 2 of the exam is split 13 for content and structure, and 12 for style and accuracy.

  •Content and Structure effectively means the interesting things you write about, and the organisation you put into writing them.

  •Style and Accuracy means the variety

of sentence structures, the wide vocabulary, and your mechanics.

## *0500-31/32/33 General Advice*

1.Read the question very carefully

2.pay close attention to what kind of writing the stimulus material is, and make a quick note of its GAWPe hats;

3.evaluate the instructions in terms of the GAWPe hats it wants YOU to wear in your answer

4.use marginal markers for every paragraph to narrate the stimulus material as you read along

5.Before you start writing your answer, you need to organise your materials. Use the bullet points as given in the question; however, the relevant points may be sprinkled throughout the insert, so you will need to gather them/mark them/colour-code them so you put the right information in the right bullet-point section.

6.Remember: STRUCTURE is very important in 0500-31.

Question 1 from 0500-31

**DO: Look at the insert and briefly read through it. Write in your notebook what its GAWP is. Now look at Question 1 and write down what GAWP you're supposed to write in for the exam.**[1]

There are several key instructions here:

•Use the bullet points as topics for each paragraph you write:

•identify skills and qualities, and evaluate them

138

•explain why you want to volunteer, and why you'd be good for the job

•(Count them, that makes 4 paragraphs!)

•Use the insert to pull out the answers to these bullet points, making sure you trawl the article for ideas that you can group into your 4 paragraphs.

•*Important Tip: The answer seems to invite you to talk about yourself, but remember that it's really wanting to know how well you have read the article and pulled out relevant points, and organised these into an appropriate piece of writing. (This is another example of the "e" in GAWPe).*

•*THIS IS REALLY IMPORTANT — If you find yourself writing a lot about your own ideas and own experience,* *you might have misread the focus of the question. There may be some leeway to reference yourself or own ideas, but the "e" in GAWPe means that the point will always be <u>more</u>about <u>pulling information</u> out of the insert , <u>evaluating </u>its information, and <u>organising</u> your answer than it will be about your own ideas.*

**DO: Read through the insert. Make your marginal markers. Now, go back through the insert a second time while looking for references to qualities and skills for the job, underlining or circling as you go. Finally, pretend like you're answering Question 3a from 0500-22, and make a list of "salient points", one list for "qualities" and one list for "skills".**

*•Important Tip: In some past papers, the task has been to evaluate opposing views about something. In that case, you wouldn't make a column of, say, qualities and another for skills, but you would put pros on one side and cons on the other.*

Now that you have found a collection of qualities and skills, it will be helpful to go through them and circle those ideas that YOU (or at least, the persona of you) could bring to this voluntary position. Jot down an example of these qualities or skills.

Finally, the fourth bullet point is about why you want to help. There are numerous reasons that you can get from the passage as to why "you" might want to volunteer.

**DO: Write down three reasons why someone would want this job, as implied in the passage.**[2]

With your Writer hat on, note your brief! According to the article, the job is to: "INSPIRE older people about computer technology and help them ENJOY it". The applicant is there in a *service* role, and the actual focus on the job is the elderly person who is there to receive support and encouragement. Don't get all high-and-mighty about how brilliant YOU are.

So, it really is important in this question to

ensure that you READ the insert carefully! The spirit of the insert can often come into play, so be sensitive to it.

Now that you have been through the insert and found the qualities and skills for the job, thought about how "you" fit into those skills, and why you want to volunteer, you are now ready to write your letter of application.

I'm often asked if it's necessary to include the full address and headings as a real letter, and the simple answer is no. If you follow the instructions and "Begin your letter: Dear Age Campaign," and finish off with a Yours Faithfully kind of signature (or even Yours Sincerely or Truly or whatever), the point is that you wrote a letter.

It's what you write in between the salutation and the closing that matters!

•Important Tip: The insert for Paper 3

*will often be about something specific, but when you come to write about them, you often need to generalise these points to fit the GAWPe of the task. In other words, taking the insert of this paper as an example, there is that quote from a specific person, an elderly woman, who is the kind of client that the Age Campaign course is aiming to help. She says that she wishes she could internet shop because she's not so mobile as younger people. Quotes like this are appropriate in articles to give opinions — that's part of their GAWP.*

*•When you come to write your letter, however, you need to remember **YOUR** GAWP! Take these special, personal, specific comments into your brain, then output them as*

something more generalised and relevant to the task. In this case, the comment about shopping was just an example given to illustrate access to vital services that are only (or more efficiently) online, and that unless the elderly get support to learn to use these resources, they feel they are losing out. It would feed into one of the reasons that you might use for the point regarding why you want to volunteer — you might think it's a shame that elderly people are being prevented from using efficient online services, simply because they don't have the confidence or knowledge for using them.

•In other words, you wouldn't actually write in your letter that you know there's a lady who can't internet shop who wants to. That's too focused on the insert and its GAWP. Be careful, however, that you're not sooooo general that you forget your GAWP, and write about helping people to use computer IN GENERAL — there are particularly issues about helping the elderly that you need to keep in mind.

Input Specifics          Output Generalisations

Here's a sample for the start of the letter:

Dear Age Campaign,

My name is Kat Patrick, and I am applying for the position of volunteer in your weekly sessions to help bring the older generation up to date with their technology skills.

In an article called "Bridging the Gap", I read that a volunteer doesn't need a great deal of experience with technology, but simply a willingness to get alongside the elderly people who are attending the course, and encourage them in their explorations on the computer. I think it's especially important to be more a listener than a talker, to find out what aspects of the computer are of most interest to the attendee, whether Facebook and other social media, online shopping, Photoshop, or simply being able to send and receive email.

*NOTICE HOW:*

•*I have focused first and foremost on the general skills needed for this position. I have trawled the insert and pulled out a variety of points, clumping them together in the single paragraph about desirable qualities.*

•*I have used the writer hat. I am being very deferential, focusing on the attendees' wishes rather than my wonderful, stupendous, unsurpassed computer skills that I would wield like a blunt object, bludgeoning my mentee with Twitter and Instagram and all sorts, when the dear little lady might only want to be able to pay her gas bill by direct debit and make a Skype call.*

<u>Reminder of the task:</u>

**Write a letter to Age Campaign, applying for a place as a volunteer in the project.**

**In your letter, you should:**

> **•identify and evaluate the skills and qualities needed as a volunteer**
>
> **•explain why you want to volunteer and why you consider yourself to be a suitable applicant**

*Do NOT write about the skills that you have, but the skills that would fit the job description the best as found in the insert. Remember that the "you" here is just a construct for purposes of the exam, though you can use your real self as a model. THEN write about why "you" want to volunteer (using the insert as guidance to what's relevant here), and why "you" think you are suitable.*

*It's the GENERAL IDEAS that you need to grasp, but don't be so general that your application could be for any job, for supporting any person. Especially be sensitive to the SPIRIT of the position as much as the details.*

### 

In Lesson Six, you've learned:

To be a very good answer for Question 1 according to the mark scheme, you need to make sure you're doing these five things:

1.organise the answer as the question paper tells you to;

2.write in the style of a letter of application within its parameters;

3.use the general points about the appropriate skills/qualities for THIS special position as found scattered throughout the stimulus material, evaluating them by giving you opinion about which are important and why

4.indicate why you want to be involved in this project, and how "you" specifically fulfil these qualities;

5.pay attention to your mechanics.

### ###

## Revision Suggestions from Lesson Six:
## Pesky Sentences
### Mechanics B

Do you know what makes a good sentence? Do you know the difference between a compound, simple, or complex sentence? More importantly, do you know the difference between a sentence fragment and a run-on sentence?

Maybe you don't know the names of these sentence differences, but you need to know when you've written a complete sentence as opposed to only part of one; you need to know when you've tried to separate two complete sentences with only a comma.

There is more information about these on the grammar workbook I referred to in Lesson 5, but here's a crash course in sentence structures.

<u>Incomplete sentence, or fragment:</u>

An incomplete sentence is one that is missing either a subject or verb, the basic building blocks of a complete sentence. You can have "he ran", but you can't have only "he" or only "ran".

Obviously!

However, most incomplete sentences are longer and more complicated, with lots of words, and yet, the subject or the verb is missing.

Example: Joey, running on empty, flagging at the end of the race.

You might not realise it, but "-ing" words aren't actually verbs. They can be adjectives or parts of verbal phrases when coupled with "was" or "were" and such, but they don't describe a completed action by themselves. For that, you need to change "flagging" to "flagged" or to "was flagging" for the sentence above to be a completed one.

Run-on sentences:

Run-on sentences are the opposite of an incomplete one: often, they are two sentences separated by a comma when stronger punctuation is needed.

Example: It's half-past five, we can't reach the town after dark now.

In the first sentence, your subject and verb are "It is", and in the second, it's "We can't reach". They are two independent sentences that can't be separated by only a comma.

Correct: It's half-past five. We can't reach the town after dark now.

or: It's half-past five, so we can't reach the town after dark now.

or: It's half-past five; we can't reach the

town after dark now.

Only by adding a conjunction (so), or by using a full stop or semi-colon, are the two completed sentences properly separated.

***Final assignment for Lesson Six:***

***DO: Write your own answer for Question 1. Be sure to follow the bullet points given, even if it feels forced. Remember not to be crass.***

# Answers

1. The answers are that the insert is an article, probably in a local paper aimed at local people including teens, an objective viewpoint with the purpose to inform; your answer is supposed to be a letter of application, written to someone who can hire you for the position, and given this GA, your writerly attitude should be formal but with some humility and tact, and the purpose is to be persuasive, not forgetting that it's "e" – an exam!

2. You may have said that you want the job to go on your CV, or that you think it's sad old people can't shop online and you want to help them do that, or that you just like being around older people because they have as much to teach you as far as life skills as you can about computing, or that you would like

the extra training that the scheme is offering, or that the article has made you think about what you take for granted and you want to give back to society, or maybe you even want to show older people that teens aren't all that bad.

# LESSON SEVEN

In this lesson, we're going to turn our attention to Part 2 of 0500-31/32/33, with a particular focus on Descriptive Writing, usually numbers questions 2 and 3. We will be referring to the June 0500-31 paper, so you need to have it in front of you during this lesson.

First. let's review what we did in Lesson Six.

- •Last time, we looked at Part 1, Question 1 of Paper 0500-31.
- •We looked at four important points about Question 1 —
  - •approximate GAWPe while still using the question's instructions re: opening sentence and using the bullet points (in the specific case of the application letter, there were two bullet points with

two parts each for a total of 4 paragraphs);

•make notes where you clump ideas or colour-code details to follow the bullet points in the task, so that you can better organise your answer;

•input                    specifics/output generalisations;

•pay attention to your mechanics.

•For revision, we explored the difference between run-on sentences and fragments.

## Overview of Part 2, 0500-31/32/33:

•Part 2 of 0500-31 contains questions 2-5. You answer only ONE of these four choices.

•2 and 3 are descriptive writing;

•4 and 5 are narrative writing.

•NOTE: In some past papers (prior to 2015), there were three kinds of writing on offer in Part 2. Since 2015, the discursive essay has been removed. However, past papers can still be useful in looking at variations of descriptive and narrative writing. Just be aware that they were then numbered 3a/3b and 4a/4b.

•Each question is worth 25 points, split into two parts:

•Content and Structure (13)

•Style and Accuracy (12).

•The key skill for Content and Structure is making the whole task stick together.

•The key skill for Style and Accuracy is your mechanics and vocabulary.

## 0500-31/32/33 Part 2, Questions 2 and 3 — Descriptive Writing

There are two key skills in a good description

•1.1 Envision the scene as a snapshot, so you avoid trying to tell a story when you're supposed to be creating atmosphere; do NOT think like a video, but a photo!

•1.2 Use the analogy of a human body – bones, muscles, and skin – to develop your description to its fullest potential.

## Step One: Envision a scene as a snapshot

It's really important to keep your Questions 2 and 3 firmly in the realm of *description* as in snapshots, as opposed to blurring them with Questions 4 and 5, the *narrative* stories, which are more like video or film, with continuous movement, rising/falling action, etc.

Let's take a snapshot and describe it in terms of just exactly what's there, without embellishing the details or adding any back story. This is sort of like "just the facts, ma'am," from the HOW hand, but in this case, it's "just the facts, ma'am" about a photograph.

**DO: Write down a list of fifteen things you see in this picture.** [1]

This kind of list-taking is what I call the bare bones of a description. It's the basis on which you will build more and more of an overall picture with atmosphere, but it's the one you begin with, just like you will start a garden with dirt, seeds, water, and sunlight, but what these create as the plants grow will change the scene enormously.

The only down-side of "bare bones", though, is that they're boring when it comes to a description. Writing an answer like this tends toward just listing details without any specific focus, and if you look at the mark scheme, that's basically Band 4 — "a series of ordinary details". Band 4 is D-ish.

As I assume you want more than Band 4 — or, at least your parents do, or they wouldn't have bought you this book! — then you need to write something more than just a barebones description, The exam wants something that connects your description together (muscles) and it want a texture, an atmosphere in it, like skin on a body.

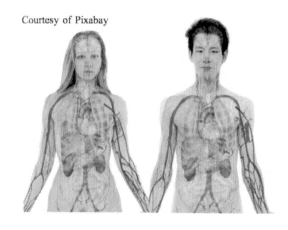

Courtesy of Pixabay

## Step Two: Put Muscle on the Bones

For example, here's a detail from the earlier

picture with the dog. The barebones of this is "dog".

If I told you simply to picture a dog, you might think of a dalmatian, a pug, a cocker-poodle-meranian pinscher. Basically, you and I would really struggle to share the same picture in our heads through simply the word "dog".

So, to convey more detail to you, I might say it's a little black-and-tan terrier with big ears. I might think of the way that its colouring is sort of like Reese's peanut-butter-cup candy. I'm adding detail, but I'm connecting the description by adding extra interest.

## Step Three: Adding Skin

Now for what I call the skin, or maybe the "texture" of the description.

See, everyone's got bones. Almost everyone's bones are pretty much the same. I'm sure you've seen the meme where there are seven skeletons, all identical, and underneath each one there's a description of someone's race: the point being made is that everyone is the same underneath, whatever colour their skin, their background, their religion.

On top of bones, almost everyone has muscle, too. Sure, these muscles do different things — a heart muscle doesn't look the same or do the same job as a thigh muscle, but they usually do the same job of connecting things together.

People's skin, however, is usually unique. There are so many different shades, and it can be hairy or smooth, it might have lots of freckles, it might be wrinkly, it will probably have scars, even if it's just from chickenpox!

Think of adding atmosphere to your descriptive writing as though you're describing skin on the muscles. Here's an example:

- The little black-and-tan terrier, the colour of a Reese's peanut-butter-cup candy, snatched the hat from the boy.
- The little black-and-tan terrier, the colour of a Reese's peanut-butter-cup

candy, licked the hat that the boy was holding.

•The little black-and-tan terrier, the colour of a Reese's peanut-butter-cup candy, dodged the boy has he tried to put his hat over her head.

The barebones of the dog, with the muscles of his colour and distinguishing details, and finally, the texture of his movements, all add together to change the atmosphere of the scene.

Snatched -- rambunctious dog
Licked -- playful or sweet dog
Dodged -- scared dog

**DO: Look at the following picture and write in your notebook a bare-bones description of it. Use a boring verb to say what it's doing. Label it "bones". Next, try to think of some way to add to its detail, such as describing its colours in interesting ways. Label this "muscle".**

**Finally, play around with different verbs to add a texture or an atmosphere to the scene. Label these "skin".[2]**

It's up to you to take the question's bare bones and turn it into a piece of writing that's full of muscle and skin.

Please note: before writing a single word, think about an overall "body" of writing. In

169

other words, don't add muscle and skin a sentence at a time, but try to come up with an overall atmosphere.

For example, our rambunctious doggy would be better accompanied by giggling children, smiling sunshine, and laughing brooks.

Our licking doggy, on the other hand, could be in a scene where everything is hungry, like caterpillars and butterflies and frogs, etc., so you give an overall view of eating.

A frightened doggy could be in a scene that's tense, with brooding clouds, threatening shadows, aggressive and nasty kids.

> •*Important Tip: Description is not simply piling up adjectives. Look at this mish-mash of descriptive words:*

"The rusty old brown door was obstructing my entrance to the gurgling, steamy laboratory that was as pitch dark and full of funny smells" is an example of immature, lazy writing.[3]

> *•There is no general feeling of atmosphere, but a hodge-podge of ideas, piled up. Instead, see how this sentence creates an atmosphere of abandonment:*

"An oak door on oxidised hinges led to a laboratory overflowing with broken beakers and seven bunsen burners, dark and disconnected."

## Question 2 of Part 2, 0500-31

**DO: Look at your exam question paper now for Part 2, subsection Descriptive Writing. We're going to focus on this one for the rest of the lesson, but before we do that, re-write the task in your**

**notebook. What do the instructions say about your beginning point? Note that there's no end point, but finishing off your description at a clear end-point is really important.**

Before you write a single word for your answer, you must — and I mean MUST — stop, look, and listen. This is a tried and true step in the process, so trust me. Make this part of your revision process, pausing to engage your brain before you engage your pen.

STOP panicking and rushing; you need to "breathe in" this scene;

LOOK around your scene – where is this

home exactly (suburbs, city centre, countryside); is it a brand new house, or only new to you; what are the smells and the sights; build up a sense of atmosphere

LISTEN to the house and its surroundings – does it creak and groan, is it solid and silent, does it keep out the noise from the street or do the sounds of a farmyard/a wood/a river invade it, enhance it, involve it?

See if you can get a sense of the kind of house that I'm describing — what is its atmosphere?

> The moment I walked into my new house, I was struck by the colour – brown everywhere. It hadn't been so noticeable before, when the previous owners had their furniture occupying the rooms, but now – empty – it all seemed a very bland

neutral shade.

The first room I came to was the lounge, where the sunlight streamed through the gaps in the blinds to make shadow-stripes on the carpet. They reminded me of a row of coffee Kit-Kat, and this gave me an idea of the cosy conversations I could have here with my new neighbours: oak nest of tables the colour of treacle, wooden coasters, over-sized mugs with steam drifting up lazily.

The dining room, however, was more like milk chocolate than coffee. Maybe that's because it had three small, square windows that made the room slightly brighter, bringing out a paler colour in the carpet than I had found in the lounge. Compare that to the dark 85% chocolate cupboards in the kitchen, there was something more-ish about the dining room, like a bar of Cadbury's Dairy Milk that begs to be eaten at one sitting. I could imagine a room as silky-smooth-feeling as this one could be hard to want to leave, especially if doing so meant a sink full of washing up next door!

So I've taken the task of describing a house, played upon the brown colour in it, and started making comparisons based on various brown foods, all comforting and cosy. Hopefully, the atmosphere of it is that it's going to be a kind of hostess-y, friendly, welcoming place.

You don't necessarily have to use fancy

words to make the point. I'm building up an atmosphere by the details I'm choosing to share, and I'm staying focused on this atmosphere. I'm not writing about one room in yellow and one room dirty and one room super huge and glossy, and then going outside in the garden to get distracted by some birds. This is a snapshot with attitude!

You may find it really difficult to make it all hang together so nicely, but if you simply make a list of important words or related words (say, for a nice house, gleaming, bright, light, shining, yellow, cheerful, solid, fresh), then you can use this list throughout the description to help the whole house have a positive atmosphere. If you want a scary house, you would choose a whole different set of words to put into your details.

**DO: Brainstorm a list of 15 words that**

**you would plant in a description of a spooky house.**[4]

Hopefully, you'll see just a little extra thought about "skin" will be the key skill that separates the mundane from the magnificent!

This technique of making a word cloud that connects is actually a literary device called "lexical field." Basically, lexical field just means word cloud.

For example, if I were to list a set of words like this –

*Fire, tripod, sleeping bag, smoke, coals, kindling, air bed, air pump, guy wires, marshmallows, hot dogs, swiss army knife, outside, starry nights*

**<u>What is the topic I'm clearly making reference to? Answer at the end of the chapter.</u>**

The way I would finish my description of the house is continuing with the reference to chocolates – something philosophical like:

> They say that life is like a box of chocolates, but in my case, it's my house that's like a chocolate box! Can't wait to dig in!"

---

### Dr P's view

To me, this should be an easy writing task. It only requires focusing on the topic, using good vocabulary and sentence structures, and controlling your punctuation. So why do students still struggle on this? SILLY MISTAKES, such as:

- Not attending to the topic (memory verse!). If the question is about the city in the early morning, don't write about it throughout the seasons, or walking into the country, or comparing the city in the morning to its night life. Answer the question as it's written!

- Over-writing. Students seem to think that piling up adjectives and imagery is good description, but the meaning of what they write might be total gobbledygook...

  - "The ratchety branch swayed lovingly in the horrific wind with birds tweeting elegantly like foghorns."

- Or (the biggest mistake of all) telling a story - thinking "video" - instead of describing something like a snapshot. There's nothing wrong with perhaps having a series of three snapshots as you move through the house or walk along the street, but if you start using words like &ldquo:when" or "then" or "next", "later that day", or even "the next week", then you are probably writing narrative, which is Question 4 or 5, not 2 and 3.

Another issue that "separates the men from the boys" is the mark scheme's expectation of organisation: it calls it "managing beginnings and endings". Students often do fine with their opening, but usually finish their descriptive piece by ... well, there's no better word for it ... abandoning it. If I'm marking a student's description and start looking for page 2 when there is none, then this piece of work hasn't been successfully brought to a close. Therefore, when planning your description, you must plan in your ending. Let's take the example of the house ... how might you bring your description of your new house to a close? Jot down five ways you can finish a description of a house you go into for the first time.[5]

---

*•Important Tip: Another problem with writing a good description is that it's easy to just list things rather than thoughtfully arrange them. You're supposed to be showing off your writing skills, remember? So don't just tell me the stairs go up and the carpet is beige and this room is a bedroom, and this room is a bedroom, and this room is a bedroom (zzzzzz....).*

*•You have to find something to give your description OOMPH! Or "X-*

Factor", and that's why I want you to think in terms of bones, muscles, and skin.

•Part of the skill of this question is choosing the better one to write about. To me, walking through a house with some kind of atmosphere (other than the obvious s-p-o-o-k-y house) is a rather dull proposition. You have to work quite hard to jazz up your description, and not just list room by room like a kind of inventory. Clearly, the morning in the city is more interesting.

•The mark scheme is looking for how well your sentences flow, how interesting your vocabulary is, and how satisfyingly contained your content is – how much it seems like an organic, thoughtful whole rather than a mish-

*mash of random ideas that are being stuffed under a single umbrella.*

*•That said, bad mechanics stick out like sore thumbs. Revise your spelling, punctuation, and grammar, as much as past papers. I mean it!*

Finally, a word about variations for Questions 2 and 3. These examples in 0500-31 are very typical: one is about <u>a building</u>, and <u>one is about a place/time</u>.

•Occasionally, you are asked to describe a person. This is a bit more difficult, but it's the same principle: think snapshots with bones, muscle, and skin. Maybe a scene with the person at breakfast, lunch, dinner. Maybe at home, work, and their hobby. "Spots of time", as the poet Wordsworth would say, rather than a film with a story-line to it.

•Occasionally, you are given bullet points to cover in your question. Remember your GAWPe, and describe according to the bullet point. Maybe you can't really establish an atmosphere in this task, so you can do two things: a) choose the alternative descriptive question!; b) brainstorm your "lexical field" of words you want to include, and pepper them through your description.

•Just remember: every task is there to give you an opening or a gateway to showing off your writing skills. The exam doesn't care whether or not you have actually gone walking in the early morning of a city, but how well you can describe such a scene in your own words with good mechanics and organisation.

### ###

In Lesson Seven, you've learned:

<u>Your 3-step approach to successful description...</u>

**plan, plan, plan**

**think, think, think**

**revise your mechanics**

*(And, add skin to muscles and bone.)*

## Revision Suggestions from Lesson Seven: Hup-Two-Three

### Descriptive Exercises

Instructions: this exercise can help you add "muscle" and "skin" to the bare bones of a description. I have given you two examples, but you can try your hand at making different atmospheres with the same scene, or find other bland statements from news stories and practise jazzing them up.

Here's a sentence from a news report from a recent newspaper article (remember, news reports are just facts, without "atmosphere"):

"Prince George and Princess Charlotte played in the snow for the first time."

Changing verbs and adding "muscle" detail and "skin" textures, this sentence can indicate different atmospheres of these scene.

a) On holiday in the resort town of Grenoble, Prince George and Princess Charlotte gambolled in the fresh powder like little spring lambs.

b) In the Cairngorms, Prince George and Princess Charlotte prodded the last patch of ice of the winter with the tips of their fingers as though they were the peas on their dinner plates that they didn't want to eat.

Hopefully, you sensed in the first one that this was rather a posh place, and the children were having innocent fun in the lovely conditions.

In the second one, the atmosphere was less enchanting. The Cairngorms might be a nice place to ski if you have to, but it's not really a nice-sounding word particularly, and is clearly down-market to somewhere in the Alps. The fact that the children were prodding ice like yucky peas, you see they're not particularly enamoured.

*Final assignment for Lesson Seven:*

*Try writing a bit of Question 2 about the new house. Remember to first STOP, LOOK, and LISTEN before you begin writing. Aim for 150 words in the first instance where you put skin on your bones and muscles. Watch your mechanics! Be careful not to drift into story-telling. It's just a series of snapshots, not a video, so you need to LINGER in your rooms, not dart from room to room. AFTER YOUR 150 WORD OPENING, SKIP A LINE AND THEN WRITE WHAT WILL BE YOUR CLOSING SENTENCE. Ask your parents if the sentence feels complete, or abandoned.*

**That list of words in the "lexical field"?**
Camping, of course! My friend says,
"Cheers!"

# Answers

1. Answers will vary, but some examples are a girl in the foreground with light-coloured hair; smiling, looking sideways, holding grass, dark jacket or hoodie; a boy in a shirt with stripes on the sleeves; dog pulling hat; boy trying to get hat; dog is little and black, maybe like a mini doberman (she's an English Toy Terrier, actually, but you weren't to know that!); the dog wears a light-coloured collar; a younger boy in the background, standing; wearing sunglass and a hat; the background is hilly with a lake in the distance; ferns nearby; a gate or fence of some kind.

2. Here is one example of how you might have answered this: Bones — a black lamb with a black-and-white-mixed face looked at me; Muscle — a black lamb with a face like

an old lady with a bad hair-dye job looked at me; Skin — a black lamb with a face like an old lady with a bad hair-dye job, glared longingly through the entrapping fence/seemed to beg me to release him from his pen; dared me to take one step closer as though he would bite my legs off.

3. By the way, I would not be impressed by this description for another reason – how can the viewpoint person know what the laboratory is like inside if the door was obstructing his entrance? THINK!

4. Some ideas: creaky, musty, groaning, howling wind, isolated, dark, dank, cobwebs, a funny chill in my bones, broken things, torn curtains, clanking, banging doors.

5. A few examples of mine: You can leave

the house. You can flop down in a room and sigh, being so glad to finally call something your own. You can close by wondering how you'll ever have enough furniture to fill it. You can make your first cup of tea.

# LESSON EIGHT

In this lesson, we're going to turn our attention to Part 2 of 0500-31/32/33, with a particular focus on Narrative Writing, usually numbers questions 4 and 5. We will be referring to the June 0500-31 paper, so you need to have it in front of you during this lesson.

First. let's review what we did in Lesson Seven.

•We looked at how descriptive writing is a focused/narrow snapshot that tries to create atmosphere through putting muscle and skin onto a skeleton of details.

•We practised important pre-writing steps:

•STOP-LOOK-LISTEN to really envision and experience the scene

193

brainstorm words, phrases, and thoughts that link to the atmosphere you want to create such as a "licking doggy" and other kinds of animals who are eating, or house that's broken, or spooky, or clean, or homely.

•We looked at the question about your new house. You practised stop-look-listen and pictured yourself in a specific place; you thought about how you might choose connected words to give atmosphere, and how you would end it without abandoning it.

•I gave an example about a new house that was very brown, but turned it into a comparison of brown-colours related to chocolate and such.

•For revision, you were given an exercise about taking bare-bones newspaper articles, and adding muscles/skin to turn them into description with atmosphere.

## *0500-31/32/33 Part 2, Questions 4 and 5 — Narrative Writing*

•Although I love writing narrative stories myself, I have to admit that this task is a lot harder than the descriptive one. That's because there's so much more to think about in a narrative story than in description.

•Descriptive writing wants to establish an atmosphere, and you do that by putting muscle and skin on your bones.

•Narrative writing needs some description in it, too, but it also adds techniques like characterisation, setting, and plot, including the important skill of creating a climax.

•More about this in a mo ...

**195**

There will be two narrative tasks to choose from in the narrative section: one task offers either a set starting point or a set end point (maybe a phrase, or an action), and the other is usually more general.

What is your GAWPe of this kind of writing?

**DO: Jot down in your notebook the GAWPe for narrative writing.**[1]

<u>Examiners have shared the following tips for this answer in public Examiners' Reports:</u>

- •Remember that stories do not consist of events alone.
- •Include realistic details, description and thoughts and feelings of characters

in the narrative.

•Try to write a narrative with a sensible time span that is not too long.

•Most poor answers are episodic rather than well-organised (I did this, then I did that), lack a good ending, and fail to capture any kind of characterisation.

•Good answers have distinctive and obvious climaxes (even surprise endings only work if they are prepared for and not sprung on the reader at the last minute); they are original, and often include some kind of brief flashback or varieties of time spans. If dialogue is included, it is well-punctuated and not overused. Characters seem realistic or at least well-drawn.

## Question 4 and 5 from 0500-31

Let's turn now to your question paper for

narrative writing. Your two choices are to write a story called The Lesson, and another story that ends, "I knew things would be different from now on."

Maybe just looking at the tasks, your brain starts churning away all kinds of cool ideas, but do take note of this bit of advice from that examiners' reports: the best answers were those which were still rooted in reality, still thinking through issues like using the senses, creating characters who were credible, and avoiding cliched situations with lots of shooting and violence as though their story were caught up in a written version of a video game.

There will be some of you will who will nevertheless think this task is a gift – you may be natural story-tellers and in your element when it comes to writing this sort of thing.

Believe me — it is a trickier task than descriptive writing, because not only do you have to be sure to include elements of descriptive writing (creating atmosphere and such), but you have to think through issues like:

- who is your narrator;
- what's your point of view;
- how do you start in the middle of the action;
- how do you prepare for the end from the beginning (without giving away your punch-line);
- who are your characters (note: you don't want too many);
- what are their motivations? their obstacles? how will they overcome them?

ACK! So much to remember!!!!

Just like you did for descriptive writing, you need to spend some time pre-writing. You begin both ways in Part 2:

STOP panicking and rushing; you need to "breathe in" the scene;

LOOK around your scene

LISTEN to the surroundings

> •Important Tip: Think before your write; picture your scene; imagine the

*atmosphere.*

*•Brainstorm! Remember Who, What, When, Where, Why, How to think through some basic ideas.*

*•If an interesting thread begins to appear as you write your story and you want to slot it into the story earlier, then use asterisks or arrows to put the idea into it. Not elegant, but acceptable.*

*•Better, however, to decide these issues in the planning stage! The exam is looking to see if you can organise you're writing, so build this skill into your answers from the start.*

I'm going to model for you the process for Question 4, called The Lesson.

I'm writing this off the top of my head. First — Stop, Look, Listen. (What kind of lesson do I want to learn, do I want to root it in an episode from my own life or make something up entirely; it would be more realistic from my own life, so what lesson did I learn – once I nearly killed my brother by pushing him over as he held an ax, and I thought he'd been killed by it like a boy in a book I read ... ok ... let's go with that lesson)

Next: Who, What, When, Where, Why, How to think through some basic ideas. OK ... my brother and I were, say, pretending to be the boys in that book. Why? That's what we used to do in the summer, before video games kept kids indoors. The "how" of it – well, we got in an argument about something which I've forgotten, so I'll have to think of a triggering event.

It's a story, so there needs to be a story arc: a beginning, middle, and end. The end is where I push him onto the ax. The beginning, we go down to the woods with some tools to play backwoodsmen. Middle needs to be the argument we get into.

Perhaps between the push and his turning out to be ok, I need a flashback to the scene where that boy is killed by falling on the ax.

I need to establish the game we're playing and the book it's based on, our ages. Perhaps I could start the story with the reference to the title, so it's clear that I know where I'm going with this episode – it's going to teach me a lesson.

My opening:

> I've heard it said in life that truth is stranger than fiction, but there was one time in my childhood days when I wish that truth and fiction had had nothing to do with each other.
>
> The year was 1980. The season was summer - hot, sticky, Texan summer. In

those days, my brother and I lived on a farm about 10 miles from town, so we spent most of our school holidays on different parts of the ranch, playing make-believe and using every inch of the fertile black soil, the fishing pond, the creek bottoms with their crawfish and water snakes.

We'd headed down that way on one particular morning, wearing jeans we'd specifically cut short to look frayed, old plaid shirts, mostly unbuttoned, and leaving our shoes at the back door. That day, we were going to be hillbilly boys like the book Where the Red Fern Grows, looking for 'coons (there weren't any) and building a bonfire.

Do you see how narrative writing is just as much about establishing atmosphere and having good words and vivid imagery as description is, but now you've got to put in more rising and falling action, you have to have a climax, you have to consider characterisation and timing.

That's not to say that it's impossible to write a good story; it's just as though there are more balls for the juggler to throw in the air than there are for description, and that's why, in my opinion, descriptive writing is easier than narrative, at least in terms of taking this exam.

That's also why, like I did for Paper 22, I suggest starting with the last question and working backwards. Remember our crazy idea from Lesson Four?

I feel as though the writing tasks of Part 2 can offer much more focused and almost formulaic responses, in a way, than Question 1 where the variations are wider. You can allow yourself 35-40 minutes for it, and do a decent job in writing a solid answer (especially a descriptive one which is more focused than narrative to begin with), thus leaving yourself a "whole heap o' time" to tackle that first question, which is no doubt trickier.

Some of you aren't comfortable with this idea, but I just want to throw that out there as an option.

**<u>NOTE: If you have liked the idea about starting backwards in your papers – say, with Question 3 in Paper 22, or Part 2 in Paper 31 – then you must practise your mocks and revision backwards as well.</u>**

•*Important Tip: I'm not going to say*

*that you can't do this narrative task, as apparently some schools say to their students. No, you might get really fired up about the task, and can't wait to tackle it. That's up to you.*

*•What I will say is this: you will need a lot of practice with regard to timing. It's difficult to crank out a story with a beginning, middle, and end, and get all your loose ends tied up by 3 pages. So, if you're going to write the narrative task, you need to practise, practise, practise.*

**Top Tip:**

Here's a good link for iGCSE revision in general, and specifically about narrative writing on p. 14 (don't worry that it talks about coursework and also that it's based on the old exam — its explanation about narrative writing is still valid). http://tinyurl.com/lmbmfav

### 

In Lesson Eight, you've learned:

•Narrative writing is like descriptive writing with more balls to juggle.

•The best way to write a successful story is to plan it out carefully before you start to write, so the ending is satisfying.

•The best way to revise for writing a story is to practise a lot of past papers, paying particular attention to your timing. You need to be able to do this within 50 minutes at the most, (unless you know you'll receive extra time during the exam).

###

# Revision Suggestions from Lesson Eight: Honing

## Revision between now and the exams

1.Don't lose sight of your fundamentals:

- •Spend fifteen minutes every day between now and then doing copywork from your chosen book and exposure text.
- •Write down the memory passage for four more times before you're done with it.
- •Practise narrating everything you read and writing markers in the margins or as notes on paper.

2.Practise makes permanent, so revise practice papers in the same time frame as you'll have in the real exam.

3.Stop using the computer and start

writing by hand, unless you have permission to use the computer in the exam.

4.Start writing with the pen you're planning to use. Black biro is best. Find a brand, size, style, that fits nicely in your hand, rolls smoothly, and doesn't give you cramp. Make sure the ink doesn't bleed through the paper, but that it will still give a strong line when scanned.

### *Final assignment for Lesson Eight:*

*DO: If you're going to leave the narrative option open for yourself in the exam, you need to get in lots of practice to perfect the timing. Go over past papers and just start cranking out stories. Beware of the cliche — remember the examiners like realistic, original work, not derivative or imitative. Try to use episodes from your real life.*

## Answers

1. Genre is narrative writing; Audience is examiner; Writer will vary, depending on the narrator/persona you choose for the story; P is usually to entertain; finally, "e" reminds us this story is for an exam, so we have to keep within its parameters.

# BONUS MINI-LESSON

This mini-lesson has only one purpose: to guide you during the 24 hours before you actually sit one of the 0500 papers.

By the time you get to the 24-hour countdown, your revision should be as complete as it can be, especially if you worked your way through this guidebook and took on board the many tips and tricks, ideas, suggestions, and advice that have made up the bulk of it.

With just 24 hours to go, your job is two-fold:

> 1.Get plenty of rest and food and exercise
>
> 2.Boost your confidence

The first is self-explanatory. The day before the exam, make sure you eat well, go for a long walk, drink plenty of water, and avoid electronics after about 7 pm so your brain can get ready to sleep (screens inhibit secretion of melatonin, which is your bed-time hormone).

The second can be achieved by a single 30-minute slot of brainstorming. What do you brainstorm? Everything you learned from this guide about the paper you're taking the next day.

For example, when that Paper 0500-21/22/23 gets plopped in front of you the next day, what are you going to find in it? (3 questions, the third split into two parts; 2 inserts) Do you have a choice of questions? (No; you answer ALL questions) What are your strategies for tackling Question 1? (Look back at Lessons 1 and 2, noticing how you should follow the bullet points in your answer, how you need to include 3 layers in the answer as in point, detail, development, and how you read into Passage A to help supply answers for your A3 section) How many points for reading well, and how many for your writing? What genres might you be asked to write in? Don't forget to pay attention to the italicised description of each piece in the insert.

After you've attended to your two tasks for the day, then there's nothing more you can do to improve your chances of a good grade. All that can be done, should have already been done in the weeks and months before.

The best thing you can do now is call your granny, if she's still alive, and tell her you love her. Our loved-ones aren't around forever, so it's only natural that we should think of them in our most trying times.

# ABOUT THE AUTHOR

Dr P runs online courses in English for home-educated students who live all over the world. Her 30-week Dreaming Spires Home Learning webinars are structured in a unique tiered format that allows 12-year-olds to get their toes wet with secondary literature, history, and writing skills, while pushing the sixth-formers to higher challenges and expectations.

Her Dreaming Spires Revision courses have proved popular since she started them in 2011. While most students are UK-based, she has also taught students in Europe, India, and New Zealand, a testament to how global the CIE iGCSE qualification truly is.

Earlier in her career, Dr P taught in the UK as a secondary school English and Drama teacher, including A-level, and also spent some time teaching university students in the US. She has also marked English exam papers.

She has four children whom she home educates using the Charlotte Mason method. This approach is dedicated to reading many, many good books, to analysis, discussion, and contextual exploration, and it underpins the vision for her online courses which her older children also attend.

In her spare time, she drives her kids to lots of swimming competitions, Scouting events, and dog shows — their little terrier is a native to the UK breed known as the English Toy Terrier. They're considered a vulnerable breed because fewer than 100 a registered every year, but being so biddable, loving, robust, and low-maintenance, she finds it surprising that they're not more popular.

Anyway, like this revision guide and the back way she gets to the NEC for the annual Crufts dog show, she likes to think of her ETTs as her own little secret.

Printed in Great Britain
by Amazon